JOHN ERICSSON

AND THE INVENTIONS OF WAR

THE HISTORY OF THE CIVIL WAR

THE HISTORY OF THE CIVIL WAR

JOHN ERICSSON

AND THE
INVENTIONS OF WAR

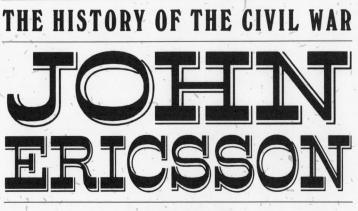

by ANN BROPHY

INTRODUCTORY ESSAY BY
HENRY STEELE COMMAGER

SILVER BURDETT PRESS

to Charles

Series Editorial Supervisor: Richard G. Gallin
Series Editing: Agincourt Press
Series Consultant: Leah Fortson
Cover and Text Design: Circa 86, Inc.
Series Supervision of Art and Design: Leslie Bauman
Maps: Susan Johnston Carlson

Consultants: Richard M. Haynes, Assistant Professor, Division of
Administration, Curriculum, and Instruction, Western Carolina
University; Arnold Markoe, Professor, Brooklyn College, City
University of New York.

Library of Congress Cataloging-in-Publication Data
Brophy, Ann.
    John Ericsson : the inventions of war / by Ann Brophy : with an
introduction by Henry Steele Commager.
        p.   cm. — (The History of the Civil War)
    Includes bibliographical references.
    Summary: Traces the life of the Swedish-American engineer and
inventor who introduced the successful use of screw propellers on
commercial and naval vessels, and designed and built the famous
Civil War ship, the *Monitor*.
    1. Ericsson, John, 1803-1889—Juvenile literature.   2. Inventors—
Biography—Juvenile literature.   [1. Ericsson, John, 1803-1889.
2. Inventors.]   I. Title.   II. Series.
T40.E75B76   1990
609.2—dc20
[B]
[90]   90-8507
    ISBN 0-382-09943-5 (lib. bdg.)   ISBN 0-382-24052-9 (pbk.)   CIP
                                                                      AC

TABLE OF CONTENTS

If asked to name the most important battle of the Civil War, most Americans would doubtless say "Gettysburg." That certainly was the worst day of the war for the Confederacy. But a very important—and perhaps even more historic—battle was that between the U.S.S. *Monitor* and the Confederate warship *Merrimack*. Although both ships survived, that battle spelled inevitable defeat for the Confederacy's naval policies and hinted at the South's final end. It meant that the Union could use a new naval technology—the ironclad—to blockade all important Confederate ports, despite strong Rebel land batteries. And it was John Ericsson who brought it all about.

Even before the battle occurred, the Union already had armored gunboats on the Mississippi. These early "ironclads" had played a decisive role in the capture of New Orleans and the reduction of the powerful Confederate fortress of Vicksburg. As the naval battles shifted to Virginia and the James River, the Confederates were the first to cover their warships with iron. Such ironclad ships were a threat to the Union fleet and to the Union armies as well.

Luckily, the navy department had the young, Swedish-born engineer John Ericsson working for it. With astonishing speed, Ericsson designed and oversaw the construction of the most powerful ironclad ship in the world. It was not just "clad," or covered, in iron, but was made entirely of iron. It also featured a revolving turret, or gun emplacement, that would prove to be one of the most devastating developments in naval history.

Who was this man who could work such genius, seemingly on demand? Ericsson had proved his genius while still a boy in his native Sweden. Fascinated with inventions and with science, Ericsson had already invented a new kind of engine, an improved locomotive, and the propellor for ships.

Ericsson left his native land to enjoy the benefits and challenges of the industrial revolution. His first stop was London, which in the mid-19th century was a playground for inventors. After a stint there, and some troubles with money—and with conservative thinkers who failed to see the wisdom in his inventions—Ericsson went to America.

It was in America that many of Ericsson's finest inventions were realized. It was not, however, until the *Monitor* was built that he was valued by a public that rewarded military victory but was slow to recognize genius. And even then, Ericsson's fame declined over time. He had either sold or failed to get patents on so many of his inventions that people ceased to identify the inventor with his innovations.

Ericsson, after leaving his native Sweden and living for a time in England, finally became a citizen in the country to whose ultimate survival and unity he had contributed so much. Though buried in his native land, John Ericsson died very much an American.

CIVIL WAR TIME LINE

May 22
Kansas-Nebraska Act states that in new territories the question of slavery will be decided by the citizens. Many Northerners are outraged because this act could lead to the extension of slavery.

| 1854 | 1855 | 1856 | 1857 |

May 21
Lawrence, Kansas is sacked by proslavery Missourians.

May 22
Senator Charles Sumner is caned by Preston Brooks for delivering a speech against slavery.

May 24 – 25
Pottawatomie Creek massacre committed by John Brown and four of his sons.

March 6
The Supreme Court, in the *Dred Scott* ruling, declares that blacks are not U. S. citizens, and therefore cannot bring lawsuits. The ruling divides the country on the question of the legal status of blacks.

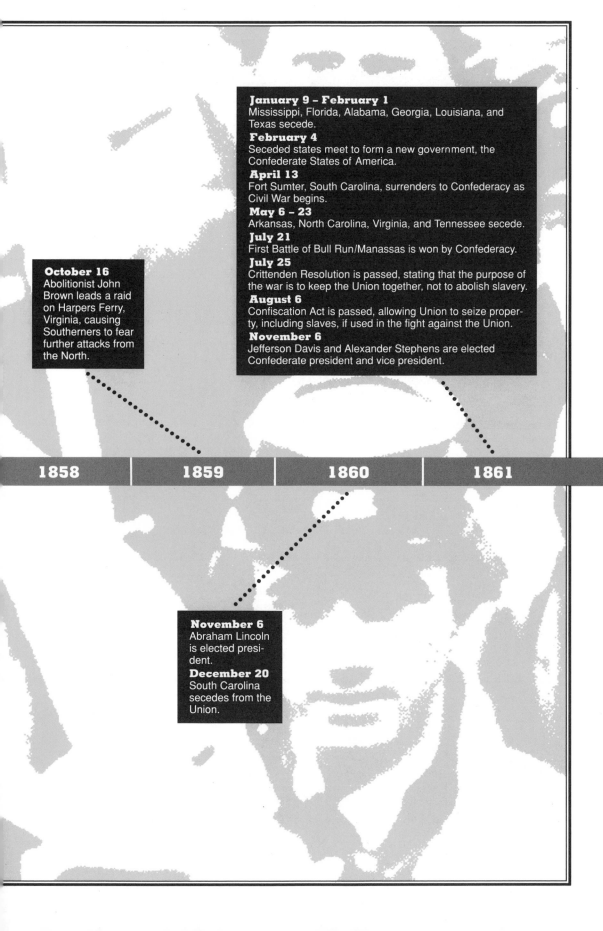

October 16
Abolitionist John Brown leads a raid on Harpers Ferry, Virginia, causing Southerners to fear further attacks from the North.

January 9 – February 1
Mississippi, Florida, Alabama, Georgia, Louisiana, and Texas secede.
February 4
Seceded states meet to form a new government, the Confederate States of America.
April 13
Fort Sumter, South Carolina, surrenders to Confederacy as Civil War begins.
May 6 – 23
Arkansas, North Carolina, Virginia, and Tennessee secede.
July 21
First Battle of Bull Run/Manassas is won by Confederacy.
July 25
Crittenden Resolution is passed, stating that the purpose of the war is to keep the Union together, not to abolish slavery.
August 6
Confiscation Act is passed, allowing Union to seize property, including slaves, if used in the fight against the Union.
November 6
Jefferson Davis and Alexander Stephens are elected Confederate president and vice president.

1858   **1859**   **1860**   **1861**

November 6
Abraham Lincoln is elected president.
December 20
South Carolina secedes from the Union.

February 6
Fort Henry, Tennessee, is captured.

February 16
Fort Donelson, Tennessee, is captured by Union.

March 9
Monitor and *Merrimack* battle near Hampton Roads, Virginia.

March 23
Shenandoah Valley Campaign opens with Union victory over Maj. Gen. Thomas J. "Stonewall" Jackson.

April 7
Gen. Ulysses S. Grant wins Battle of Shiloh, Tennessee, splitting rebel forces on the Mississippi River.

April 25
New Orleans is captured by Union naval forces led by flag officer David Farragut.

June 19
Slavery is abolished in U. S. territories.

June 25
Gen. Robert E. Lee leads rout of Gen. George McClellan's army in the Seven Days Battles.

July 17
The United States Congress authorizes formation of the first black regiments.

August 29 – 30
Second Battle of Bull Run/Manassas is won by Confederacy.

September 5
Lee leads first Confederate invasion of the North into Maryland.

September 17
Battle of Antietam/Sharpsburg, bloodiest of the war, ends in a stalemate between Lee and McClellan.

1862　　**1863**　　**1864**　　**1865**

January 1
Lincoln issues Emancipation Proclamation, freeing slaves in Confederate states.

March 3
U.S. Congress passes its first military draft.

April 2
Bread riots occur in Richmond, Virginia.

May 1 – 4
Battle of Chancellorsville is won by Confederacy; Stonewall Jackson is accidentally shot by his own troops.

May 22 – July 4
Union wins siege of Vicksburg in Mississippi.

June 3
Lee invades the North from Fredericksburg, Virginia.

July 3
Battle of Gettysburg is won in Pennsylvania by Union.

July 13 – 17
Riots occur in New York City over the draft.

November 19
Lincoln delivers the Gettysburg Address.

March 12
Grant becomes general-in-chief of Union army.
May 5 – 6
Lee and Lt. Gen. James Longstreet defeat Grant at the Wilderness Battle in Virginia.
May 6 – September 2
Atlanta Campaign ends in Union general William Tecumseh Sherman's occupation of Atlanta.
May 8 – 19
Lee and Grant maneuver for position in the Spotsylvania Campaign.
June 3
Grant is repelled at Cold Harbor, Virginia.
June 18, 1864 – April 2, 1865
Grant conducts the Siege of Petersburg, in Virginia, ending with evacuation of the city and Confederate withdrawal from Richmond.
August 5
Admiral Farragut wins Battle of Mobile Bay for Union.
October 6
Union general Philip Sheridan lays waste to Shenandoah Valley, Virginia, cutting off Confederacy's food supplies.
November 8
Lincoln is reelected president.
November 15 – December 13
Sherman's March to the Sea ends with Union occupation of Savannah, Georgia.

March 2
First Reconstruction Act is passed, reorganizing governments of Southern states.

1866   1867   1868   1869

April 9
Civil Rights Act of 1866 is passed. Among other things, it removes states' power to keep former slaves from testifying in court or owning property.

November 3
Ulysses S. Grant is elected president.

January 31
Thirteenth Amendment, freeing slaves, is passed by Congress and sent to states for ratification.
February 1 – April 26
Sherman invades the Carolinas.
February 6
Lee is appointed general-in-chief of Confederate armies.
March 3
Freedman's Bureau is established to assist former slaves.
April 9
Lee surrenders to Grant at Appomattox Courthouse, Virginia.
April 15
Lincoln dies from assassin's bullet; Andrew Johnson becomes president.
May 26
Remaining Confederate troops surrender.

THE DREAMER

"We are such stuff as dreams are made on."
WILLIAM SHAKESPEARE,
The Tempest

 little boy sat alone on a mountainside in Sweden. He was studying the tall pine trees, the lights and shadows of the surrounding forest, and the mist hovering gently over the Swedish streams. He was glad it was summer again, and the long, dark winter months had passed.

His brother, Nils, and his sister, Anna Carolina, were too busy playing to notice him. They also knew enough not to bother him. They knew that he would never join them in foot races with the other children or in paddling on rafts in water races. He had far better things to do. He had to think and study and try to understand the wonders of the natural world. He seemed much older than they were, even though he was the baby of the family. He had more questions, more curiosity, more impatience to learn. There was so much to the world, so many people making so much happen. He wished to be one of those people. And 50 years later, in a battle that took place far across the ocean, John Ericsson's wish would come true.

But for now, why did the mist rise from the earth on a hot summer afternoon? Why did trees grow in one place, and not in other places, to make a forest?

13

How did the fish propel themselves through the clear water?
What caused the flowers to reach for the sun?

That evening at supper he would ask his father, and his father would answer his questions.

John admired his father for being so smart. Olaf Ericsson had graduated from a college in Karlstad, the principal town of the province of Vermland in Sweden. He had been trained in science and mathematics, and had a talent for working with machinery and tools. He came from a family of serious, well-to-do miners who worked hard, loved their country, and believed in a firm code of ethics. In 1799, at the age of 21, Olaf Ericsson married Brita Sophia Yngström, a Flemish girl his own age. She was fun-loving, an ardent reader, and very beautiful. She also came from a family of miners and landowners in Vermland.

As their three children were born, Olaf continued the family tradition, working as a mine inspector in the Vermland mountains that rose high and handsome behind their farmhouse. The mountains were rich in deposits of iron ore, and the deep iron mines provided the family with a good but hard-earned living.

When John and Nils would visit their father at the mine, John would make drawings of all the machinery, and he would ask any number of questions:

How did the pulley work?
How was the size of the gears determined?
What made them move around and around?
Why was the drill stronger than the rock?
Why did the rock break apart in just the right place?

One day John's father showed him the power of heat by suspending a small glass tube containing water over a bright flame. John never forgot the excitement he felt as he watched the water bubble into steam. This simple experiment proved to be the basis for John Ericsson's lifetime work.

In 1811, when John was eight years old, the mechanical corps of the Swedish navy decided to build a great canal that would run through the middle of Sweden. The canal would divide the country

Highlights in the Life of John Ericsson

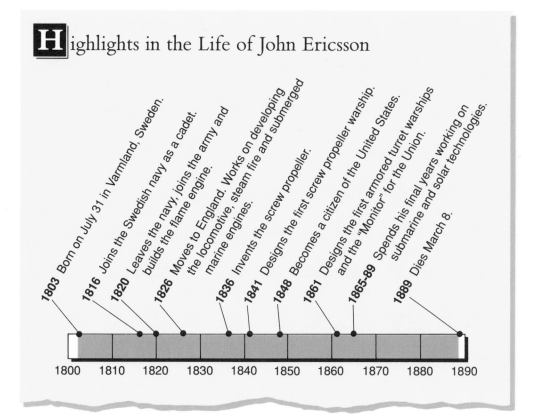

1803 Born on July 31 in Varmland, Sweden.

1816 Joins the Swedish navy as a cadet.

1820 Leaves the navy, joins the army and builds the flame engine.

1826 Moves to England. Works on developing the locomotive, steam fire and submerged marine engines.

1836 Invents the screw propeller.

1841 Designs the first screw propeller warship.

1848 Becomes a citizen of the United States.

1861 Designs the first armored turret warships and the "Monitor" for the Union.

1865-89 Spends his final years working on submarine and solar technologies.

1889 Dies March 8.

1800   1810   1820   1830   1840   1850   1860   1870   1880   1890

into many rivers, lakes, and busy waterways. It was a very ambitious project, and John's father was appointed chief blasting engineer for one section of the canal.

To do this job, Olaf Ericsson told his family that they would have to move to Forsvik, a hundred miles away. John's mother packed up all the furniture, clothes, copper pots and pans, her many novels, and her Bible pictures. Anna Carolina packed up her rag dolls. Nils packed up his models of mine machinery and his sled, his skates, his bows and arrows, his raft, and his fishing gear. John packed up his drawing board and all his questions. Off they went to their new home on the shores of Lake Vattern.

John was happy there. He could watch firsthand the construction of the Göta Canal. Things he had only dreamed about were now becoming real before his eyes. He began to draw designs for the canal and to construct models of the machinery and tools that were used in its construction. These models were not a child's attempt at copying; they were actual working models. He constructed a sawmill. He built a pump for the mill from pieces of wood, a watch spring, and a broken tin spoon, and he watched with great delight as the water turned the wheel and it began to move. Much later in his life, when he was asked what mechanical achievement he considered to be his best, the tiny sawmill and pump headed his list.

During the summer days when his family left home for picnics and play, John waved goodbye to them and returned to work at his drawing board. He also sat before his drawing board late into the long winter nights copying and perfecting his plans. He was never pushed or forced to excel. He went simply and quietly about his work as if it were play, because for him the science of motion was the greatest toy.

But most of all, he was happy because as yet there were no schools in Forsvik. He would not have to sit in stuffy classrooms

listening to teachers talk about history and Latin and French and other subjects that did not interest him.

Instead, he was tutored by his father and other engineers in subjects he did like: drawing, mathematics, and English. He also studied chemistry and learned to make his own inks and colors. In this environment, he was able to practice his lessons every day and apply his knowledge in a practical way. Later in his life, he said that if he had gone to a regular school he would "have had such a belief in authorities" that he "would not have dared to develop originality."

John made windmills out of watch springs, and drawing brushes out of the fine hairs from his mother's fur coat. He made compasses out of birch wood with sewing needles attached to the ends. By the time he was 14, he had developed plans and models for many inventions. And he always tried hard to do more things and better things than his brother, Nils.

Nils did not mind. He was happy, too. He always did as he was told, and he never questioned the ways things were. He was entirely content to follow the beaten path. He did his job well, and when he was finished he put it all behind him. In the summer, he practiced archery and went fishing and sailing. In the winter, he took his iceboat skimming across the frozen lake by the side of the house and raced on snow shoes across the white crusted fields. There was usually a crowd of friends following close behind him.

John always felt that his parents favored Nils—Nils was far easier to manage. Nils never made a mess around the house with his drawing boards and papers. He never raided his mother's sewing basket for pins and needles, and he never emptied his father's tool box all over the kitchen table in a search for just the right piece of metal.

Forsvik proved to be an important place for John's early training. The chief engineer at the Göta Canal was a man named Count Baltzer Bogislaus von Platen. The count was so impressed by the talents of the nine-year-old boy and his ten-year-old brother that he appointed them both as cadets in the mechanical corps of the navy. As cadets, the boys worked and were trained to become officers of the navy.

Nils worked for four years as a carpenter and a cement maker, but John was sent to the map division for only six weeks. He went back to his drawing board, and his maps became an important part of the direction of the canal. He also made a drawing of the Sunderland iron bridge. This drawing was so perfectly executed that the count put it on permanent display in his quarters. He referred to John as his young prodigy.

"Continue as you have begun," the count told John, "and you will one day produce something extraordinary." John listened to the count's words and never forgot their promise.

When he was 13 years old, John was promoted to assistant leveler. He was responsible for deciding which flat surfaces to use for blasting and was put in charge of 600 men. It did not bother John that he was much younger and much smaller than his workmen, nor did it bother his workmen. They admired the teenage boy who had to carry around a platform to stand on in order to see through the surveying lens.

John was well-liked at the canal, and for the first time in his life he made friends. He had had two promotions since his family had come to Forsvik five years before. He was making about $24 a month for his family, and his father was proud of him. He was living out his early dreams.

He could even answer many of his own questions now. However, he found that with each new assignment he had new questions, and his father was still there with the answers. Then one day in 1818, because of failing health and overwork, his father died at the age of 40.

Until that day, the family had lived well. In addition to his earnings, John's father received money from inherited land holdings. Brita Sophia had all the latest in cookware and the very best clothes. Anna Carolina had the most beautiful dresses and dolls. Nils and John had the most modern tools. Now their father was gone, and the money was gone, too.

Immediately, John's mother took charge. She was a strong woman. Because she was a very good cook, she decided to take in

boarders to add to the salaries of her sons. Anna Carolina helped her mother, and soon the Ericsson boardinghouse became the popular meeting place for military officers who had come to work on the canal.

The officers who sat around the Ericsson supper table were not satisfied with life as it was. They were energetic men of ideas, curiosity, and knowledge about the universe. They thought that life could be better and that there were many more things that needed to be done. They knew, for example, that there were basic laws about the energy needed to heat water. They wondered if that energy could be used—in the form of steam.

They also talked about a branch of the Swedish army whose troops lived on land in the country's far northern regions. Along with their usual military duties, these troops experimented with new engineering and construction ideas. It was a great new world out there, said the officers who came to the Ericsson boarding house. A world to be conquered with flames and swords—and imagination. It was a world that would not stand still.

John grew more and more excited with each passing meal, and between bites of codfish stew, potato dumplings, and boiled cabbage, he made up his mind to resign from the navy.

When John, who was now 17, told Count von Platen of his plans, the count tried his best to discourage him. He reminded John that he had achieved an outstanding reputation in the navy. He could look forward to a promising career. John only shook his head.

He thanked the count for everything he had done for him. He told him how much he appreciated the opportunities, the experiences, and the knowledge he had been given, but he said that it was time for him to move on.

Finally, in anger, the count told him to "go to the devil."

John went to the Swedish army instead.

THE SOLDIER

"Always inventing, designing, constructing"
SAID ABOUT JOHN ERICSSON BY ONE
OF HIS SUPERIOR OFFICERS

 ricsson was sent to the Twenty-third Rifle Corps of the Swedish army, far, far north, just a few miles south of the Arctic Circle.

His regiment was stationed in Jemtland, a mountain district 200 miles north of Vermland. It was a region filled with lakes and rivers that were frozen solid from October to June. In summer, many wooded islands could be seen in the lakes. Rivers of melting ice cascaded down from the highest mountains in Sweden into the valleys below.

The climate in Jemtland was sunny and the soil was rich. Farmers and cattle thrived on the land during the summer months. The midnight sun shone brightly for almost 24 hours each day. But the winter months turned the land into a dark, barren wilderness. Many boys John's age would have found life there depressing and dull. But John found it exciting. It was something new and different, and he looked forward to each new experience.

He quickly became a skillful gunner and devoted himself to the science of artillery, which he studied with great enthusiasm. His many questions now were about guns, and he studied hard until he could answer them all. He was especially concerned with putting bigger and more powerful guns on gunboats. He found that his navy background came in very handy. This enthusiastic approach to naval gunnery would later lead to the most notable achievement of his life.

He was "exceedingly active," one of his superior officers said, "always inventing, designing, constructing."

After his first seven weeks of military training, he wrote to his mother, "I have learned tolerable well what it means to be a soldier and am inspired with an unchanging love for the military profession."

He also developed another, more personal interest. At this particular time in Sweden, a scientific system of gymnastics was introduced by Henrick Ling. It was based on the study of anatomy, the structure of the human body. The idea of the system was to build better and stronger bodies.

Ericsson, who had never been active in sports, decided that this new idea was a good one. He especially liked the scientific approach that it took.

He read all about such men as the first Christian king of Norway, who "could keep five daggers in the air, always catching the proper fifth by its handle, and sending it aloft again; could shoot supremely, throw a javelin with either hand; excelling also in swimming, climbing, leaping." John was determined to equal these feats, and very soon he did.

He became known as the Hercules of his regiment, breaking all records in wrestling, leaping bars, and lifting weights.

One day he lifted a cannon weighing 600 pounds. This ambitious act proved too much for an 18-year-old boy, and he suffered from a bad back for the rest of his life. But he had proved something to himself. He had proved that he could do anything, if he wanted to do it badly enough. And this thought that anything was possible became one of John Ericsson's lifetime beliefs.

It was also around this time that Ericsson became interested in young women. There were many daughters of officers around, and Ericsson found one whom he particularly liked.

Carolina Lillieskold's father was one of John's superior officers and a nobleman. She was a beautiful young woman who was popular with many of the soldiers. But after meeting John, she forgot all the others.

Ericsson was a handsome young man, with curly brown hair and broad, muscular shoulders. He took pride in the way he looked and dressed.

He found himself writing love poems to Carolina now, instead of working on his scientific studies. He wrote to his mother that he was "by no means inexperienced in the language of feeling." John and Carolina became engaged to be married.

A short time later, however, Carolina's father insisted that the engagement be broken. Swedish custom did not encourage a marriage between a poor lieutenant and a woman of noble birth. Carolina left home for a trip to Stockholm where, in 1824, she gave birth to a boy, John Ericsson's son, and placed him in a foster home before returning to Jemtland. Then she married according to her father's wishes. Carolina never made any attempt to find her son by John Ericsson. John did not meet his son until 50 years later.

After his sad and short-lived affair, Ericsson returned to his work with a vengeance. Except for seeing a few good friends, he no longer had any social life. He decided to write a book about his experiences working on the Göta Canal. Once again he spent many long nights at his drawing board, studying the sketches and mechanical drawings he had accumulated during his service under Count von Platen. He described the machinery, the tools that were used for canal work, the locks, and the methods of transportation at that time.

When he had finished, he asked for a leave of absence and took the book to Stockholm to have it published. At that time, the art of printing drawings was still new. When Ericsson asked to see the engraver's equipment that would be used to print his drawings, the publishers refused to reveal the secrets of their craft. They told him that his demands were impossible and to go away.

So Ericsson went home and decided to invent his own engraving equipment and to publish his own book. Within a year, part of the book was published in a Swedish illustrated magazine. "I remember very well the surprise of certain engravers," Ericsson later said.

He soon had to put the book project aside because of his military duties, but he had once again proved that he could do anything that he really wanted to do.

Perhaps Ericsson's most important achievement in the Swedish army was to win a nationwide competition to become the government surveyor for the northern region of the country. The assignment was to measure the land and make maps of the area. He won easily over many more experienced and older soldiers. The pay for this project was based on the amount of work done and Ericsson chose to go on the payroll as not one, but two, people. This double duty was worth the effort. The maps he made received much notice, and the extra money he received made his first famous invention possible. This was the flame engine.

Ericsson remembered the time his father had shown him the power of steam—water turning to a vapor over a flame. Once again, he began asking himself questions:

Why did the heat cause motion?

Would hot air also cause motion?

Would hot air be able to drive an engine?

Would air power be equal to and less expensive than steam power?

He answered yes to all these questions, and right away he set about to prove his point. Other men had advanced hot-air theories, but they had never fully explored them. One of these theories was that air could be heated to a high enough temperature to equal the engine-driving properties of steam. This theory particularly interested Ericsson, so he constructed a machine that he called the "caloric engine" or the "flame engine." He found that the theory of hot-air power worked. The engine produced several horsepower, and it opened the door to other possibilities. He asked himself more questions.

What if there were a larger volume of hot air?

What if that larger volume were compressed into a smaller area?

What if the engine were made larger?

What if the engine could move something really big?

He began to dream again. He dreamed of a great mechanical revolution. He dreamed of inventions that had been talked about but never built. He dreamed of being the one to make them work.

In 1826, at the age of 23, he wrote a paper about his caloric engine entitled "A Description of a New Method of Employing the Combustion of Fuel as a Moving Power." He promptly sent it to the newly formed Society of Civil Engineers in London.

Ericsson was growing less interested in military life. His interest now was totally in scientific things, and he became impatient with the duties of a soldier. Again, he felt that it was time for him to move on.

One of his fellow officers wrote at the time, "I could not bear the thought of his genius burying itself in Jemtland. I advised him to go to England."

Unfortunately, Ericsson had spent all of his money on the flame engine. He could not afford to make a trip to England. His fellow officers asked how much he would need to start out. Ericsson answered that he could go if he had a thousand crowns—about $500.

Ericsson's many admirers in the regiment collected the money and gave it to him as a present. He obtained a leave of absence from the army, and, after many farewell parties, he left Sweden.

He promised to return as soon as his flame engine was successfully delivered, but the opportunities in England proved too great. Ericsson would never again live in his native land.

GOINGS-ON IN EUROPE

"It was a magical machine which dragged us along the rails."

A PASSENGER ON ONE OF THE FIRST
LOCOMOTIVE TRAINS IN ENGLAND

John Ericsson was not alone in wanting to move on. The Industrial Revolution was at hand. Society was looking toward a wide use of machinery and operations in industry and commerce on a grand scale to supply the needs of everyone. Local markets were looking for worldwide connections, and people were no longer content to sit still. They wanted to see the rest of the world. They wanted to travel. In order to do all these things, they had to make greater use of machinery. They had to develop greater sources of power.

England was the first country to begin this change, and with good reason. England was already engaging in free trade within its boundaries. There were no government regulations on goods, which could be carried back and forth with ease and without cost. The political situation was stable there because of a clearly defined and accepted class structure. England also had special markets in Canada and its former colonies, the United States. Most of all, England was rich in the natural resources of iron and coal—important materials for building and moving machines. By 1830,

England was producing 80 percent of Europe's coal and 50 percent of the continent's iron. Almost all of the steam engines in Europe were made in England.

The other European nations lagged behind England in the Industrial Revolution. France was England's greatest economic rival, but France could not keep up with the production of its rich neighbor. Italy had no coal or iron. Holland was at a disadvantage because of its small population. Spain clung to the glories of its history, and Russia remained a nation set apart from these changes.

England welcomed inventors for their ideas and business people to help get the inventions built. England recognized the value of machines.

At the beginning of the Industrial Revolution, machines were run by water power, but this method soon proved too slow for a rapidly changing way of life. Coal became the chief source of energy. Inventors turned to coal to provide the great heat needed in the furnaces and hearths of the many factories that were being opened.

Textile mills developed under the power of coal. The "old fashioned" water-powered shuttle and spinning frames of the 18th century were exchanged for the "modern" coal-powered machines of the 19th century. Fabrics were turned out at twice the former speed. By 1837, there were 85,000 power looms in England. The woolen and cotton industries were a major source of goods to sell in other countries.

Canals were built to open waterways from the coal fields to the cities and the seaports. Faster transportation became a reality with the invention of the paddle-wheel steamboat. These revolutionary boats with wheels of wooden paddles were used on all the European canals in 1826. One of the them, the Dutch vessel S.S. *Curaçao,* even attempted to cross the Atlantic, but had to turn back because of lack of fresh water for the steam boilers. In 1838, however, the British steamships S.S. *Sirius* and *Great Western* left England and arrived safely in New York less than three weeks later. This was the first time that ships powered entirely by steam crossed the Atlantic.

Two years later, Samuel Cunard, a British civil engineer, won a British contract to supply regular transportation service from Liverpool, England, to Halifax, Nova Scotia, and then to Boston. The wooden steamship *Britannia* also sailed that year. The Peninsular and Oriental Maritime Company started routes to Asia and later to Australia. New markets for manufactured goods were opening up all over the world. Machinery and goods had to be moved. So did people. At the beginning of the 18th century, one-third of the entire naval power of Europe had belonged to England. It was not until 1750, however, that shipbuilding establishments in that country were able to overcome the rigid restrictions that the government had set up to control the size and construction of a warship. In 1757, a new class of frigate was constructed. It was a large two-decker ship, 176 feet long on the gun deck, and it carried between 30 and 40 cannon. There was ample room for officers' cabins and hammock berths for the crew. There were also storerooms for food, fresh water, ammunition, and supplies, and an adequate galley. It took about 4,000 loads of timber to build a ship of this size. A mature oak tree could provide enough wood for one load.

The hull design of the sailing warships was also improved. The square bow was rounded. This provided more shelter for the crew. The circular stern was introduced, allowing more space for guns. The construction pattern was also much stronger. In 1827 the circular stern design was further altered to an elliptical shape, which permitted extra gunports aft and projecting walkways. At the beginning of the 19th century, the British navy had more than 200 of these frigates in commission, each carrying approximately 500 men. They continued to be among the most important and useful units of the European sailing navies at that time.

On land, the railways were expanding at an equally fast rate. The Stockton and Darlington Railway opened in 1825 with the first steam locomotive passenger cars. The trains traveled at the amazing speed of 12 miles an hour. One member of Parliament said that it was "unthinkable to move at 12 miles an hour with the aid of the devil in the form of a locomotive."

A drawing of an early locomotive, which moved at the "devilish speed" of 12 miles per hour.

Other railways soon followed. In 1830, the Liverpool and Manchester line opened for business. It boasted both freight and passenger service, and people rushed to get aboard. One of the first passengers said, "It was a magical machine which dragged us along the rails. I felt as if no fairy tale was ever half so wonderful as what I saw."

A short time later, a young engineer named Isambard Kingdom Brunel built the Great Western Railway, complete with iron bridges. There was opposition to this expanding rail system, however. Farmers asked high prices for the land that the railway companies needed to buy. The canal owners protested the noisy railroads. Still, England was fast on the move across both land and water.

The world's first wire suspension bridge was built near Lyons, France, in 1825. London's Hammersmith Bridge, the world's first suspension bridge constructed of stone and metal, was completed in 1826. The roadways of suspension bridges were hung from thick cables that were stretched from one end to the other.

The idea of mass public transportation was first introduced with the horse-drawn omnibus. This proved to be the beginning of the modern bus system. These crude "buggies" traveled on smooth,

THE EXPLOSION OF TECHNOLOGY

The mechanical innovations of the 19th century affected every aspect of life. From simple, everyday inventions like the typewriter to the enormous steam engines that powered ships and locomotives, everything moved faster and made more noise. No individual could remain untouched by this swift expansion of technology, and though many feared it, there were also advantages. The sheer human drudgery that was once required in nearly every stage of manufacturing was eliminated in many industries. Machines assured uniform and speedy production of articles that were once difficult and time-consuming to make. Commerce boomed, because it took far fewer employees to make many more things. In a few decades, the world would be transformed by inventions large and small.

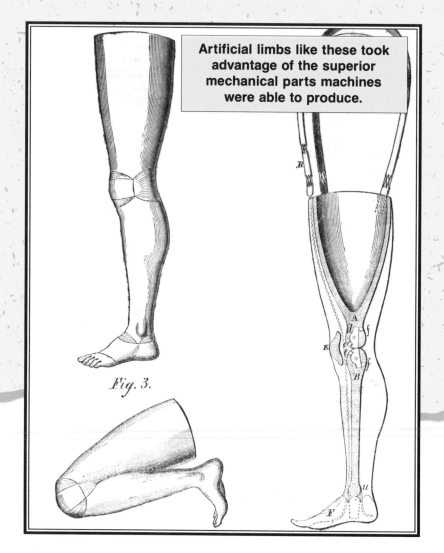

Artificial limbs like these took advantage of the superior mechanical parts machines were able to produce.

Fig. 3.

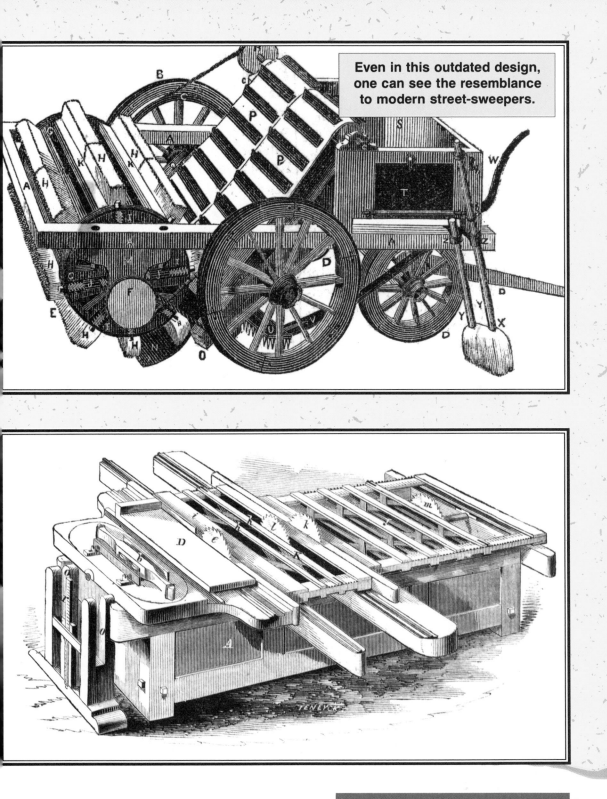

Even in this outdated design, one can see the resemblance to modern street-sweepers.

This machine is a prime example of an innovation that replaced complicated manual labor.

"macadam" highways instead of on dirt roads. A Scottish engineer, John McAdams, had invented this process for making roads. Layers of small broken stones were covered with tar or asphalt to hold them together. This was the beginning of today's paved highways.

However, all of these industrial changes brought about alarming social results. People were now able to enter into commerce and make a profit. People now had a chance to travel, to invest, and to buy the many goods the revolution made available. A popular publication of the time put it this way: "Two centuries ago, not one person in a thousand wore stockings. One century ago, not one person in five hundred wore them. Now, not one person in a thousand is without them."

Competition was keen, and people were greedy. More and more factories sprang up in every small town, and jobs became plentiful. Farmers left their fields and hurried to the towns, where they were promised good wages. The towns became terribly overcrowded with this great increase in population, and suddenly there were slums. There were homeless people, too; they filled the parks and slept on abandoned boats, under arches and in alleys and doorways. Children searched for pieces of iron that were left behind by barges in order to sell them for a few pennies. Other children worked in factories or coal mines or as chimney sweeps. Charles Dickens, whose novels were often set in industrial cities, described such a city this way in his novel *Hard Times:*

> It was a town of red brick, or of brick that would have been red if the smoke and ashes had allowed it; it was a town of machinery and tall chimneys, out of which interminable serpents of smoke trailed themselves for ever and ever, and never got uncoiled. It had a black canal in it, and a river that ran purple with ill smelling dye.

Until 1829, when Sir Robert Peel established a police force in London, enforcing the law was left to the occasional night watchman or guard. Not until the Factory Act of 1833 were inspectors appointed in an effort to bring accidents, disease, and brutal treatment of factory workers to an end.

The workers established trade unions in order to protect themselves against the demands of the employers. With the unions came strikes, in which working people tried to get better pay or conditions by stopping work. With strikes, there was the possibility of more people without jobs. It was difficult to satisfy all the people in this mechanical society, and hardship often resulted. Life had changed too fast. People were having trouble keeping up with the times.

England suffered the most, because England was more intensely industrialized. Later on, other European countries were able to watch and study England's mistakes and therefore avoid some of the same difficulties.

France had some important industries, but it remained mainly rural. Germany had a large peasant population and still looked to farming as a main support. Scotland was also rural, and aside from making better Scottish roads and bridges, it was content to improve farming. The first workable machine that cut grain was built there. The many Scottish inventors of this time usually moved to England to live and work.

The basis for all these achievements in the Industrial Revolution was the valuable use of machinery. Machines were making machines, and suddenly anything became possible. All that was needed was someone with an idea. John Ericsson had plenty of ideas.

OFF TO ENGLAND

"[He] saw things not as they are, but as they should be."

WILLIAM CONANT CHURCH
Life of John Ericsson

hen John Ericsson arrived in London on May 18, 1826, he had a head full of ideas, a heart full of hope, and a pocket full of money. He did not have quite as much money as he had received from his friends, because he had gone to many parties the previous week in Stockholm. The heir to the Swedish throne had just been born, and Ericsson was only too happy to celebrate the occasion. Besides, he was 23 years old and suddenly free from military demands. He was in complete control of his own life for the first time.

He was also full of self-confidence. After all, he had the substitute for the steam engine among his luggage. His paper on this caloric engine, which ran on hot air instead of water, had been received with much excitement in Sweden. The new engine was more efficient and less dangerous to operate. Ericsson hurried to show it off in London. He made an appointment with the Institute of Civil Engineers. The historian Ruth White described the scene:

Without apology for his youth or the Scandinavian lilt to his speech, he spoke rapidly in an alien language which had been mastered in all but accent … The sounds jarred on British ears as sharply as the words he used with less pedantry than most men of his day. The total effect created was of a self-confident, handsome young upstart from Sweden, not seeking approval of his betters, but clashing audaciously against the stronghold of their ideas.

The Society of Civil Engineers took an instant dislike to the arrogant young man who had descended upon them to shake up their comfortable beliefs. John Ericsson was not asking questions now. He was telling them how things should be done.

He showed them an engine designed with a cylinder containing a small flame. The flame heated the incoming air and expanded it to move the pistons. The pistons then drove the machinery. The air would circulate through a series of pipes and return to the cylinder without any loss of intensity, which occurs with steam. "Action will be hastened and fuel economized," he promised, "without the danger of boilers exploding under heavy steam pressure."

Unfortunately, those words proved to be wrong. For his demonstration, Ericsson used British coal inside his engine instead of Swedish pine shavings. The different coal caused such intense heat that the entire engine was destroyed. Ericsson was humiliated in front of his colleagues.

That was the end of Ericsson's association with the Society of Civil Engineers. That was also the end of his money. In addition to living in good quarters, he liked to eat well, and he had spent a great deal of money on custom-made clothes in Stockholm. Assembling and displaying his flame engine had also been costly, and he had counted on it to make him some money. Instead, it had left him penniless. He did not even have enough money left to travel back to Sweden.

Although surprised and disappointed by his first major defeat, Ericsson put the flame engine aside for the moment and decided to work on another idea.

London was full of new inventions. Horse-drawn omnibuses crowded the now-paved London streets. The first mail deliveries were made at an astounding speed of 11 miles an hour over the English countryside. Paddle steamers were on many of the European waterways.

Steam had always intrigued Ericsson, and he followed the progress of steamship theory with great interest. William Symington, a Scottish engineer, had produced the first steamer to be used in a practical way. He had successfully towed two vessels down a canal in 1801.

At the same time, Robert Fulton was experimenting in France, and in 1803 he successfully navigated his steamboat on the river Seine in France. Four years later, Fulton traveled with his steamboat, the Clermont, from New York to Albany—a distance of 120 miles. Then, with the outbreak of the war in 1812, he produced a steam man-of-war, the Demologos. It had two hulls with a paddle wheel between them. Sparks and flames erupted from its funnel, which was placed immediately in front of the wheel, and viewers considered it both awkward-looking and dangerous. The British navy, although it had adopted the use of steam for small craft such as tugs, had quickly rejected steam power for its warships.

The French navy, however, felt differently. The French had fewer ships, and they readily decided to convert those ships to steam. By 1822, General Paixhans, a notable French artillery officer, had foretold the coming of steam propulsion and explosive shells. France could surpass the hesitant English and gain supremacy on the seas. The British were faced with a very vivid threat, and during the next 10 years they were forced to experiment with steam-driven warships.

At first the proposition of adding steam-power to sailing vessels was acceptable. But when the navy tried to convert the larger ships of the fleet entirely to steam it ran into difficulty. The only means of propelling a steamship at the time was by using paddle wheels, and the paddle wheels presented a problem. These wheels, placed in boxes, protruded from either side of the hull, and they were extremely vulnerable to cannon fire. They also required a great deal of space that could be better used for the ship's own cannon. Such ample space should not be sacrificed for such fragile devices as

Robert Fulton's steamboat drew reactions of surprise and horror from those who witnessed its maiden voyage.

paddle wheels. So, it was not until 1830 that the British navy provided these vessels with guns, and they first appeared on the list of the navy as men-of-war.

In the meantime, John Ericsson was working on his theory of using caloric power to move large ships. The British fleet of 200 paddle steamers seemed old-fashioned to Ericsson. These steamships should move more swiftly, he thought. They should not be hampered by both wheels and sails. They should be moved by caloric power. So, in spite of the government opposition that he faced, Ericsson set about to improve the British navy. As the historian William Church wrote, "John Ericsson saw things not as they are, but as they should be."

Ericsson toyed with the idea of a gas engine. Then he returned to his old idea of the flame engine, but with one important improvement. He would place the flame directly under the piston, and the expanding air would supply the power. This one simple idea of compressed air was the key to a whole series of future inventions. Compressing the volume of air in a contained space would cause the air to expand when it was released. As it turned out, Ericsson's faulty first attempt to display his flame engine was not a failure after all. He had learned from his mistake.

In 1819, a vessel named the *Savannah* had crossed the Atlantic Ocean, using steam power for part of the trip. It was the first time that a ship had made such an ambitious voyage. Ericsson read about this revolutionary feat at the time, and he felt that now was the time to improve upon that success. He would develop smaller and lighter boilers that turned hot water into steam. By increasing the heat, he would then increase the power and speed.

He remembered well that particular moment when he was a child in Sweden and his father had shown him the power of heat. He remembered how excited he had been to actually see what could happen. He was grateful to his father for showing him that simple experiment a long time ago. Now, in England, the opportunities to apply his engineering skills seemed endless.

Since he had spent all of his money, he would have to figure out some way to remain in this promising and advanced country. He would have to find a job.

NEW FRIENDS

"Great, good fortune"
JOHN ERICSSON, ON GETTING
HIS FIRST JOB IN LONDON

It was with "great, good fortune," Ericsson said, that a job found him. And it found him quickly.

John Braithwaite was the owner of an old, established engineering firm in London. He was in desperate need of a partner who would help him deal with the ever-increasing demands for steam engines and air pumps. He had been present at Ericsson's failed attempt to promote his flame engine, but he had been most impressed with the young man's "flaming personality and talent." Soon the sign over the firm's door read "Braithwaite and Ericsson."

This proved to be the perfect place for Ericsson. The firm manufactured machines, and John Braithwaite was open to new ideas.

Ericsson felt he needed to make up for the recent failure of his flame engine. He went to work immediately. He spent long days at the foundry, and in the evenings he walked the London streets to clear his mind and think up new projects for the firm. Often he would stop in for a quick drink in one of the public houses, or pubs. It was in one of them that he met Felix Booth, the owner of a brewery. Booth became the first customer of Braithwaite and

Ericsson. They supplied Booth with his first pumping engines. The device was Ericsson's first steam-powered fire engine, standing slim and proud in the brewery yard, ready to squelch any flames that might threaten the brewery.

For the next 10 years at the foundry, from 1826 to 1836, Ericsson was able to put more of his plans into practice, and John Braithwaite was able to take most of the credit. Ericsson worked on a machine that would draw salt out of water and a depth-finder for ships. He also worked on furnaces, a machine for weighing liquids under pressure, and a machine to raise water from a mine shaft. He used the theory of compressed air to transmit power. He patented more than 30 inventions. (A patent is a government record of an invention that gives a person the sole right to use and sell the invention for a period of time.) Most of the patents on Ericsson's inventions were in John Braithwaite's name.

It became a very profitable partnership for the older man, while the younger man was gaining much valuable knowledge. He later said: "In the various mechanical operations we carried out together, I gained experience which, but for the confidence and liberality of Mr. B., I probably never should have acquired."

Still, Ericsson did not become a businessman. He was a dreamer, and far too involved with ideas and inventions to make money from his dreams. He did not pay attention to the actual practices of business. Now, once again, he found himself in financial trouble. His only way out was to "sell" his ideas to the men who could produce them, and he did this for the rest of his life. As a result, he never received the proper credit or fame that he so rightly deserved, or the financial rewards that he so badly needed.

Ericsson's total involvement in his work caused another problem. He had forgotten that his army leave had run out. Consequently, he was now listed as a deserter. With the help of friends in Sweden, however, he was quickly reinstated in the army and raised to the rank of captain. He accepted this promotion with gratitude, and, just as quickly, resigned from the army the next day. But he proudly bore the title of Captain John Ericsson for the rest of his life.

While John Braithwaite remained his friend and partner, Captain John Ross became his friend and advisor. Captain Ross had one thing in mind. He wanted to find a northwest passage. The British were seeking a water route across the northern part of North America that would make it possible to travel more quickly from the Atlantic Ocean to the Pacific Ocean. In 1829, the British Admiralty offered a large sum of money to "any person or persons who shall discover a Northwest Passage through Hudson Strait to the West and South Oceans of America." The passage was never found, however. It did not exist.

Captain Ross had attempted to find such a passage without success. When he offered to try again, the government refused his offer. He then went to a friend, Felix Booth, who introduced him to John Ericsson. By this time Braithwaite and Ericsson were supplying refrigerators and coolers for most of the London breweries and distilleries. What had started as a simple visit to a London public house years before had developed into a thriving business for the foundry. Felix Booth was greatly impressed with the young inventor, and he was only too happy to introduce him to all his friends.

Captain Ross was also impressed with Ericsson's inventions, and he promptly ordered one of his boilers to accompany a marine engine on an old paddlewheel ship called the *Victory*. He did not tell Ericsson that he was planning another attempt to cross the freezing Arctic seas. Ericsson believed that Ross was merely experimenting with a future warship.

Ericsson moved ahead with his usual enthusiasm. To the marine engine, he added another of his inventions. He called it his "surface condenser." This idea came from his experience in dealing with breweries and distilleries. He would adapt the same machinery that condensed, or changed, steam into water in his fire engine to condensing steam in a ship. Ericsson also decided to place the machinery below the water line.

Captain Ross was grateful and excited by this addition to this ship, and it was only after Ericsson had completed his changes to the vessel that he found out the destination. Ericsson was skeptical. Ross was eager to get started.

Felix Booth promised to sponsor the expedition, and Captain Ross's voyage of discovery was under way. Unfortunately, when the *Victory*, with its huge underwater paddles and an enormously heavy cargo, sailed through sheets of floating ice, the engines broke down, and "the great, original and glorious idea" of plowing the Arctic fields by means of steam came to an abrupt halt. Ericsson's method of condensation did not work with salt water. When greater steam pressure was applied to increase the speed, the engines became clogged with salt.

Captain Ross blamed the entire failure on Ericsson. Ericsson replied that he had not been told the purpose of the voyage. He was only experimenting, he said, and "in experimenting, complication is not regarded, since the intention generally is to ascertain facts and effects never known, for guidance in future practice." He also wrote a letter to Captain Ross charging him with an "utter forgetfulness of justice and candor." Felix Booth had to come between Ross and Ericsson to prevent a duel from taking place.

Ericsson returned to his drawing board and perfected the surface condenser. This machine condensed steam by shooting jets of cold water into the steam-containing cylinder or boiler. For the first time in marine history, the boiler worked successfully below the water line. This surface condenser is still used today in steam power plants.

Captain Ross continued his vendetta. He charged Braithwaite and Ericsson with "gross neglect," but the charges did not amount to a solid legal case. The British Admiralty had already formed a negative opinion of Captain Ross. It had formed an opinion of John Ericsson earlier, but that opinion would eventually be changed for the better, along with the entire future of naval construction.

If Ericsson's financial and professional life during this period was not successful, his personal life was. He met and married Amelia Byam in 1836. He was 33. She was 19. She was a stepsister of his friend Charles Seidler, a German shipbuilder who had introduced steamships on the Rhine River. Byam came from a distinguished English family that had settled in the West Indies. Ericsson had visited her often at the Seidler home. He called her "intelligent, generous in disposition, cultivated and very handsome." Amelia was 14 years younger than Ericsson, who sometimes worried that he might lose her to younger and more eager boyfriends.

Amelia was a talented musician and loved good books. Ericsson loved music and reading, too. She was well-educated and very social. She was the perfect hostess, and Ericsson learned to be the perfect host. He enjoyed the company of others for the first time in many years, and they often entertained their many friends.

The couple moved to the best address in London and lived a life they could not really afford. They both firmly believed that his inventions would support them. But inventing took time, and Ericsson never knew whether his inventions would be accepted and produced. He also never knew for sure whether he would be paid for his work.

As time went on, it seemed that Amelia did not share Ericsson's interest in his work. Day after day, she was left alone while her husband pursued his dreams. In the evenings, he returned to his habit of taking long, solitary walks through the London streets, gathering his thoughts for the next day's work. Soon, he and Amelia drifted apart.

Looking back on his marriage of 30 years, Ericsson later said, "I have not been in church since March, 1826, except once in London, when on a certain morning I committed the indiscretion of not only going inside the holy room, but of also appearing before the altar and there giving a promise difficult to keep."

In London, Ericsson had come up against his wife's lack of interest in his inventions. He also had to face another obstacle—British society's reluctance to accept new ideas.

Old Ideas

"The great lightness of the Novelty, its compactness, its beautiful workmanship, excited universal admiration."

Mechanics Magazine, 1829

n August 1829, John Ericsson received his first real break. It also turned out to be an unwelcome introduction to the established order of England.

The firm of Braithwaite and Ericsson heard of an engine contest to be sponsored by the Liverpool and Manchester Railway. The details of the desired engine were described with care, and the rules of the competition were exact. The engine should weigh not more than six tons. It should use up its own smoke. It should travel at 10 miles an hour. It must have two independent safety valves. The boiler must be supported on springs at a specific height. The steam pressure must be an exact amount, and the engine must be completed and ready to go by October 1, 1829. The government officials agreed on the specifications, but they did not like the impossible speed of 10 miles an hour. They felt that this was much too fast a pace for an unproved method of transportation. However, George Stephenson was the engineer of the railroad, and he insisted on the contest. His son, Robert, would be one of the chief competitors.

John Ericsson would also compete. Although he did not have such an engine ready, he quickly went to work to produce one. The prize of £500 was too good to pass up. In just seven weeks he had built one, and his locomotive, the *Novelty,* was ready for the Rainhill Trials.

On the morning of October 6, 1829, the scene at the railway station at Kenrick's Cross in Lancashire looked like a Derby Day and a circus combined. Spectators had come from miles around. They traveled by horse, by foot, by cart, and by wagon. They traveled by everything except the dreaded railroad. A reporter from the London *Times* estimated the crowd to be at least 10,000. It was a day of brightly colored flags and shawls and handkerchiefs, banners and caps. "Never," reported the *Times,* "on any occasion, were so many scientific gentlemen and practical engineers collected to-gether at one spot." The air was filled with anticipation, and five "iron monsters" were on the tracks. One of these iron monsters was George Stephenson's *Rocket.*

The *Rocket* was a large, solid, awesome locomotive, twice the weight and size of the *Novelty.* Perhaps because of this fact, the *Novelty* picked up its speed to an unheard of 30 miles an hour and easily won the first race. "The great lightness of the *Novelty,*" recorded a reporter from *Mechanic's Magazine,* "its compactness, its beautiful workmanship, excited universal admiration." The *Rocket* had traveled at the speed of 24 miles an hour. This was considered by the officials as a good speed, much safer and more acceptable. They clearly favored the *Rocket.*

On the second day, the *Novelty* and the *Rocket* were the only competitors left. This time the *Novelty* speed was clocked at almost 31 miles an hour. All the judges grew uneasy, since the Stephenson name was well regarded in railway circles, and the Ericsson name was nothing but a threat. They wondered how a man who was only 26 years old could surpass the work of England's most famous locomotive engineer.

The answer was simple. Ericsson had created the *Novelty* from ideas that had been successful in his earlier inventions. The boiler design came from his ill-starred polar vessel *Victory*. The spring-mounted machinery was inspired by the springs on his fire engine, as was the light frame.

The judges were in a quandary. Somehow they had to stop the *Novelty*. When rain forced the judges to postpone the final day of the contest, they used the additional time to set forth a whole new set of rules that would disqualify the *Novelty* and assure victory for the *Rocket*. These rules created a run of 70 miles to be accomplished on $1^3/_4$ miles of track, forcing 20 trips back and forth. Stephenson knew of the change in rules ahead of time, and he was able to adjust his engine for the turning around. Ericsson did not know about the rule change, and he lost precious time.

When Ericsson and his friends protested, Stephenson accepted his prize graciously by saying that "the locomotive is not the product of any single man, but a nation of engineers."

The historian William Conant Church wrote that this was "a weary world for those who see much beyond their fellows." It was also a weary world for a country that failed to see into the future.

There were two other questions to be considered, the government said. How would a locomotive travel up and down a hill? And what would hold its wheels on the track? John Ericsson had the answers to these questions, too. But now, he realized, it would take a long time to get anyone to listen.

England was prejudiced against "easy" travel, and speed would make travel easier. It would open up a way for the public to go places where only a favored few had gone before. It would place the peasant and the person of high rank on the same level, and England was a proud land that clung to its traditional ways. Transporting goods in a faster manner might be all right, but transporting masses of people in this way would be a serious mistake. And, after all, there were canals for the transportation of goods.

"Journeys at that time," said James John Garth Wilkinson, an influential landowner, "were restricted to a small portion of the community. The more the coaches were perfected, and the better horsed, the more expensive and select they became. To move the rich needed only a four-horse coach, but to move the poor required cars before which those of the triumphing Caesars must pale their ineffectual competition."

In other words, many Englishmen at the time would have said that it was far better and much less expensive to keep the poor at home, still reading by wax candles instead of gas lamps.

Once again, fame and fortune had eluded Ericsson. He was never particularly good at getting the credit he deserved for his inventions. And he was unable to manage money well enough to develop his new inventions independently. He would have to share the rewards of his work with those who would finance the inventions.

So, after the disappointing Rainhill Trials and the continuing negative attitude toward railroads, Ericsson decided to lay aside his creative plans for land travel for the moment. He would concentrate once again on travel by sea.

He was helped by his friend Francis Ogden, who was appointed by the United States government to look for business opportunities in Liverpool. With Ogden's encouragement, Ericsson was able to put his most advanced invention into practice. This was the screw propeller, which would run a ship all by itself without the aid of clumsy paddlewheels.

Francis Ogden planned to equip a tugboat with Ericsson's screw propeller. He also planned to have the tugboat accompany the Admiralty Barge, which was the supreme ship of the English navy. The Admiralty Lords, the most important naval officers, would all be aboard. With some reluctance, the Admiralty Board accepted Ogden's invitation. The river Thames was the site of this historic trip.

As the small tugboat steamed along, pulling the large barge at the astounding rate of 10 miles an hour, the crowd of onlookers broke into applause and called her the *Flying Devil*.

The Admiralty Lords were far less enthusiastic. They considered it "their bounden duty to discourage to the utmost of their ability the use of steam vessels, as they consider the introduction of steam calculated to strike a fatal blow at the naval supremacy of the

Empire." They simply did not understand the idea behind Ericsson's invention. Besides, next to the Admiralty Barge, the *Flying Devil* looked like a "peasant." They were used to a ship "drifting with the current, guided by a long oar." This new revelation was definitely not "out of a maritime age of grace and beauty."

Ericsson considered the trip very successful. The boiler had not exploded. The *Flying Devil* had gone faster than any other ship its size. The tugboat moved like a fish in the Swedish streams—by unseen rear propulsion.

However, the Lords merely shook their heads in disbelief and scorn. They thanked Ericsson for showing them his creation, said that they appreciated the "expense and trouble," but said that they considered the whole idea "useless, absolutely impossible." They were happy and satisfied with the navy as it was and had been for many years. There was no need for change.

The "expense and trouble" that the Lords had mentioned threw the firm of Braithwaite and Ericsson into bankruptcy. The company could not pay all the money it owed. Ericsson ended up in debtor's prison, a dreary jail in downtown London.

It was painfully obvious that many of the English Lords resisted speed. Speed was dangerous, and steam power meant speed. They even disliked moving carriages by steam over English highways, which were now paved. They would rather concentrate their efforts and money on improving the breed of carriage horses instead of encouraging invention.

Ericsson realized that those who opposed change in England were afraid of anything that might disturb the current social structure. So he put aside his efforts to improve the transportation systems. He decided to experiment with something that would not threaten the class system. He went back to his steam fire engine. He thought that the time might be right to move it from the brewery yards out into the streets of London.

Until this time, fires had been fought with what one writer of the time called "diverse squirts and petty engines to be drawn upon wheels, from place to place, for to quench fire among buildings."

Two sets of men sat on a hand engine, operating a flexible hose that was stuck into a hole they had torn in the street. Through the hole they were sometimes able to gather water, but more often they gathered stones and dirt.

Three times, London had almost been destroyed by fire. John Ericsson felt that a good, solid steam fire engine was just what was needed, and that it would not offend anyone. He was wrong again, however.

Ericsson's steam fire engine worked perfectly for five hours in putting out a large fire that threatened downtown London. However, the London Fire Brigade said that "it was too powerful for common use, too heavy for rapid traveling, and required larger supplies of water than could be obtained in London streets." They added that "even if the steam fire engines could get water, it would not be desirable to use them, as the quantity of water thrown by them might be injuriously applied and cause mischief."

Finally, in July 1860, the London Fire Engine Establishment accepted and used the first land steam-run fire engine. It was praised for its "efficiency, simplicity, durability of parts, weight and cost." It was similar to John Ericsson's fire engine, but John Ericsson was not around to see it. He had left England for the United States 21 years earlier in the hope that a new country would be more open to new ideas.

GOINGS-ON IN THE UNITED STATES

"America, the land of unlimited possibilities"
LUDWIG MAX GOLDBERGER

The United States was ready and waiting for anything new when the widespread wave of immigration from Europe reached its shores. As Americans moved to the West in search of land and gold, Europeans crossed the Atlantic Ocean and took their places in the East.

The immigrants came for many reasons, but mainly they desired freedom of expression and an opportunity to advance their personal interests. The United States was looking forward. It was an inventor's paradise.

There were 3,300 miles of canals in the United States, and more canals were being completed every year. Steamboat service was thriving. Of the more than 2 million tons of goods to be shipped, 60,000 tons were shipped by steam. People were also traveling by steamboats, back and forth on the numerous waterways. The United States was not afraid of steam. Steam was welcomed as a way to move both people and merchandise. And in the 1830s, the United States had an abundance of both.

However, the United States Navy had come to a standstill. The 1820s had been peaceful years and, except for attempts to control piracy in the West Indies and slave trade at home, the navy really had nothing to do. The Board of Navy Commissioners was made up of aging veterans of the War of 1812, and they were content to let things be. Conservatism was now their doctrine, much as it had been the rule of the Admiralty Board in England in the 1820s. After all, the United States did boast three of the largest and finest frigates that had ever been built. The *United States* and the *Constitution* had been launched in 1797, and the *President* had set sail in 1800. These ships measured 204 feet, and, although they were called 44-gun frigates, they actually carried 52 guns. They were 20 feet longer than the French ships. And they had proven to be the fastest warships afloat.

The navy decided to stay with its frigates and cruising ships. Cutters—very small sailing vessels—were also popular to pursue smugglers, and they were kept intact for use as light cruisers or as dispatch boats in the event of war. In 1831, the navy purchased two schooners to act as guards of the timberlands, but they were hardly warships. They were small and each one carried only one gun. There was a definite shortage of small vessels in the navy, and it was too costly to maintain the large ones.

In 1833 and 1834, Congress made additional funds available to the navy, which decided to build a brigantine line—an improved and updated version of the previous schooners. One of these brigantines, the *Dolphin,* launched in 1836, was considered to be one of the fastest sailers in the navy and lasted until the outbreak of the Civil War.

The last sailing frigate designed for the United States Navy was the *Congress,* launched in 1841. That ship represented the highest development of the frigate class in the United States and proved worthy of high esteem, until it was sunk in the battle of Hampton Roads in Virginia, in 1862. Ironically, this battle saw the introduction of an entirely new form of warship, Ericsson's own ironclad, *Monitor.*

Finally, in 1839, Congress set up two navy boards. One of these was composed of senior naval officers and the other one was made up of shipbuilders and an engineer. The old ideas for warships were fading with the advent of steam power and Robert Fulton's steamboat, and the idea of fortifying hulls with iron was slowly beginning to be realized in the shipyards.

Agricultural life was also on the move. The horse-guided McCormick reaper was introduced by Cyrus Hall McCormick in Virginia. Its revolutionary dividing blade and mechanical fingers separated, cut, and stacked stalks of grain. Now the work of five men could be done by one. John Deere produced steel plows with curved blades to match the curves of the land. The first steam-powered threshing machine was introduced in Maine. It separated the kernels of grain from the stalks and allowed food to be produced more efficiently and quickly.

The textile industry was on the move, as well. In Massachusetts, the power loom was weaving carpets, and in New York, the two-threaded sewing machine was making clothes. Wool production thrived in Vermont, where sheep were plentiful, and the new machines were eagerly accepted. Charles Goodyear invented the first effective use of rubber for clothing and shoes, by treating the raw material so it would not melt.

Transportation in America was undergoing a revolution, both on water and on land. The United States welcomed steam locomotives. Railways covered 2,816 miles of land, with more than 300 railroad companies in operation. The first American-built locomotive was shown by Peter Cooper. It was called the *Tom Thumb,* and was used to prove that a train could move around sharp curves. An industrialist, Matthias William Baldwin, introduced his Baldwin steam locomotive, which traveled at the astounding speed of 62 miles an hour. He was hailed as a genius. Seth Baldwin was at work on improving steam locomotives and standing steam engines. Isaac Dripps perfected the first cow-catcher, a metal frame put on the front of a locomotive to clear the tracks.

There were also many other inventions being made that affected every aspect of life. The Colt 6-shooter pistol was invented in Hartford, Connecticut by Samuel Colt. A chemically treated match was devised in Springfield, Massachusetts. The magnetic telegraph was patented by Samuel F. B. Morse. It used a series of dots and dashes called the Morse code to send messages.

In medicine, a welcome form of anesthetic called chloroform was developed by the chemist Samuel Guthrie. It allowed a patient to sleep during an operation to avoid suffering pain. The dangerous disease called cholera was brought under control by new medical developments.

Bottled sparkling water was sold in New York by a former Englishman named John Matthews, and the popular soda fountain was established. Thousands of newspapers were founded, and the first American dictionary was published. Colleges were established. Department stores were built to take the place of the small country stores of the past. Banking houses and other business firms opened their doors, and opportunities for employment were as numerous as opportunities for developing dreams.

All over the country, industry was booming and people were on the move. There was no stopping now or looking back. The United States was decidedly the land of the future. It was the place to be.

During the 1830s, 60,000 immigrants arrived each year at New York harbor. John Ericsson was one of them.

OFF TO THE UNITED STATES

"Captain Ericsson, we will make your name ring
on the Delaware!"

LT. ROBERT STOCKTON,
UNITED STATES NAVY

Ericsson sailed into New York harbor on November 23, 1839. Behind him lay 13 years of frustration and more than 100 inventions that had been dismissed by English authorities. Behind him also lay a list of patents that had never been registered in Ericsson's own name, and a break with his former partner, John Braithwaite, who had taken the credit for many of Ericsson's inventions. Nor did Mrs. Ericsson come with her husband on the trip that would take at least 20 days aboard ship. She was used to comfort, and travel by ship in those days often meant discomfort and even danger. So Ericsson left his wife behind.

What he did take with him on his voyage across the Atlantic was his collection of drawings and his "Oregon" gun. This gun was equipped with self-acting gun locks that enabled it to fire shots in rapid succession. He also took with him the admiration and faith of a new friend named Robert Stockton.

Robert Stockton was a lieutenant in the United States Navy who had been visiting in London. He was a well-bred, educated man with a head full of advanced theories, a charming manner, and fiery speaking skills. Perhaps most important of all, Stockton had a pocketful of inherited wealth, in addition to political ambitions and friends in high places.

By Francis B. Ogden's invitation, Stockton had witnessed the *Flying Devil*'s performance on the Thames. He had been greatly impressed by Ericsson's invention, traveling at the speed of 10 miles an hour without the use of sail or paddle. He did not care about the British Admiralty's negative reaction. "I do not want the opinions of your scientific men," he said. "What I have seen this day satisfies me."

Stockton remembered well how British ships had blockaded American shipping in the War of 1812. The United States Navy had done well in the war, but Stockton knew that it could and had to do even better. He immediately recognized John Ericsson as a man who thought the same way. Stockton placed an order in England for one of Ericsson's steamships to be delivered to the United States.

"Captain Ericsson," he declared enthusiastically, "we will make your name ring on the Delaware!" He planned to place a gun on a merchant ship that would be fitted with self-acting locks, so that the pitch of any waves would not upset the gun. He would call the ship the *Stockton,* and it would completely change the United States Navy.

Ericsson was elated. He immediately went to work, and the *Stockton* was launched in England on July 7, 1838. This ship was small but neatly conceived, and its iron hull was sleek and trim. It was a credit to its designer. Ericsson was even more elated. He aimed to build a "a glorified *Stockton,*" a battleship unlike anything yet conceived by the naval architects of the world.

Such a ship would be safe against enemy fire, and it would be quite indestructible. He had carried Robert Stockton's dream one step further. Now it was Stockton's turn to be elated. The ship, he declared, would be called the *Princeton.*

When Stockton returned to the United States, he wrote Ericsson a letter telling him that the United States Congress had agreed to the construction of three warships. Two of these ships were to be equipped with steam paddles, but the design of the third ship was as yet undecided. Stockton remembered a conversation about iron-

The U.S.S. *Princeton* was the most powerful steam warship of its day.

hulled warships, and he insisted that Ericsson draw up plans for a 2000-ton ship and bring the plans to the United States. Delighted, Ericsson went back to his drawing board, and eight months later he sailed for America.

What he first saw in New York pleased and inspired him. Tall sailing ships lined the shores of the Battery, overlooking New York harbor. Crowds of people were running about, loading and unloading wares on the docks, calling to each other in many languages. There seemed to be no class system here, no unnecessary ceremony, no need to worry about convention. There was an excitement, a constant motion, a sense of speed. Ericsson felt right at home.

He went immediately across the East River to the Brooklyn Navy Yard, where, at Robert Stockton's invitation, he was commissioned to test his gun.

After settling into a low-cost boardinghouse in Brooklyn, he was told that Stockton was off on another one of his political campaigns and would be unable to push ahead with plans for the *Princeton*. In addition, Stockton would be unable to sponsor Ericsson's stay in the United States. Stockton was sorry, but his own personal ambitions had called him elsewhere. Ericsson was sorry, too, but he also had personal ambitions. He moved across the river into the very expensive Astor House.

Ericsson chose this particular lodging for two reasons. It was located near the Phoenix Foundry, where he had taken the *Princeton* model. But more important, it was the home of many literary, political, and professional men, and he was stimulated by their company. They talked about many things, though politics seemed to be the favorite topic. Almost every conversation would conclude with a discussion concerning the future of this "new" country.

Ericsson sensed much unrest in the United States. A financial panic in 1837 had thrown the country into chaos. Banks no longer had enough gold to back up their bank notes, and employers were forced to pay workers with nearly worthless paper money. The land of "great opportunity" was experiencing a great depression.

Ericsson thought back to his time in England. There were always those people who would cling to the past, but at least in the United States the government itself was new enough to listen to the present. The present, however, seemed much too changeable, and the government seemed to be too inexperienced.

One of Ericsson's circle of friends at Astor House was the United States senator from Massachusetts, Daniel Webster. Nine years earlier, the senator had given a speech in reply to one by a senator from South Carolina, Robert Hayne. Hayne had threatened that the South would leave the Union. Their debate was over the rights of states and the high tariffs, or taxes, that the North had placed on Southern goods. Daniel Webster's voice rang out in defiance: "Liberty and Union, now and forever, one and inseparable!"

Webster and his friends talked about that speech, and they talked about a growing concern over a divided country. The North had many industries. The South depended primarily on farming. What would happen if the North and the South could not come to terms? The word "war" was not actually spoken, but it was in all their thoughts. They were interested in Ericsson's point of view. They encouraged his ideas, and they were impressed by his theories and dreams of the future.

Ericsson received his first order for machinery in the United States from Russell and Stephen Glover, two New York shipbuilders. They wanted two of Ericsson's small screw propeller steamboats.

Ericsson was ready. Perhaps he had studied the theory of Archimedes, a Greek mathematician of many centuries before. This ancient inventor was ahead of his time, much like Ericsson. He had invented a machine for raising water by using a cylinder and the threads of a screw.

John Ericsson's revolutionary screw propeller was dismissed as "useless" by the British admiralty.

Carrying Archimedes' theory further, Ericsson cut a screw in half and tilted it at an angle. Then he turned the screw and watched as water was pulled into motion. If water was set into motion, then a ship could be set into motion, and people could be carried into motion. All this could be done by some underwater instrument, far below the water line, that nobody would see. It would be almost like a ghost ship, moving by an invisible force—a most effective and frightening battleship. Its model, the *Princeton,* was sitting at the Phoenix Foundry just across the street.

Cornelius Delamater owned the Phoenix Foundry. He agreed with Ericsson that the *Princeton* was the ship of the future. Delamater decided to sponsor Ericsson. It was a partnership that became very profitable, and it proved to be the only lasting friendship that Ericsson ever enjoyed. The unhappy result of Ericsson's first business venture with John Braithwaite was only a bad memory now, and he no longer needed to depend on Robert Stockton.

Cornelius Delamater was a worldly man much younger than Ericsson. Still, he looked after Ericsson like a father. This friendship gave Ericsson the freedom to develop his work without having to worry about money. This was perhaps the most pleasant time of his life, and it was surely the time when John Ericsson attained his greatest achievement.

THE PRINCETON AND THE PEACEMAKER

"May it not bear the sword in vain, but be a
terror to evildoers."

ROBERT STOCKTON,
ON THE LAUNCHING OF THE PRINCETON

While Ericsson was discussing the future of American politics at Astor House, his former sponsor, Robert Stockton, was fighting what seemed to be a losing battle with Congress. Stockton had established himself as a strong supporter of the Whig party. The Whigs were the conservative politicians, the ones who opposed change and protected tradition. Stockton felt that this position would enable him to voice some control over the Southern Democrats. After all, he was a fiery public speaker with an appealing manner. He was known for being a person with new ideas and the means to carry them out.

However, when President William Henry Harrison died, John Tyler took his place, and Robert Stockton took leave of the Whig party. Stockton did not trust a Virginian as president; he felt the Whigs had made a bad mistake in selecting a southerner as vice president. Although President Tyler wanted Stockton to be secretary of the navy, Stockton did not accept the offer. He saw more opportunities for himself outside the confines of Washington politics. He quickly took his old uniform out of the closet and returned to active duty in the United States Navy.

His first call was on his friend John Ericsson. He told Ericsson about those two steam warships that the navy had ordered. He told him how they had been launched successfully and how more engineers were needed for their operation. That third warship, he said, was still open for bidding, and he still thought the third warship should be Ericsson's screw-propelled ship. Now was the time for the *Princeton*.

"Captain Ericsson," he bellowed, "our cause is assured!" Then he added in confidential tones, "I need not tell you how great an effort had been made to procure our ship." The word *our* stuck in Ericsson's mind, but he said nothing.

"Can you give me now, very roughly mind you, an approximation of dimensions and costs?" Stockton went on.

Ericsson hesitated while he thought. "I believe we may submit as maximum a sum of $75,000."

Stockton smiled, and his voice boomed. "Excellent! We will put it down at $100,000 to make ample provision for the use of your patents."

At this point, Ericsson repeated two mistakes he would make again and again throughout his life. He seriously underestimated how much money he would need, and he failed to protect his rights as the owner of his own inventions. He said, "Let us not place our plan in jeopardy. You may tell the Navy commissioners that $75,000 will suffice. I freely waive my patent rights for this experiment." Robert Stockton must have known what Ericsson was giving up, but he said nothing.

So, Ericsson, in his usual naïve way, went gratefully ahead and produced the first iron-hulled warship, with a screw propeller. The hull was built in the Philadelphia Navy Yard, and the engine was built in New York. Ericsson traveled back and forth between these two cities in a frantic effort to direct the building of his inventions first-hand. He wanted to make sure that nothing went wrong, and Stockton had told him that "time is of the essence." The United States Navy must be prepared in case of war.

Unfortunately, during this wild activity, Amelia arrived from England to be with her husband. She had been encouraged by his letters, telling her of his recent accomplishments. He had also sent her large amounts of money from time to time, whenever he received payment for his work. She was looking forward to being with him again. But what she found at the Astor House was a room cluttered with papers, letters, and drawings. She did not find her husband. She did not even find space in which to unpack.

Soon they moved to a large mansion that they once again hoped to pay for with money John would receive for his inventions. Amelia still did not have space for herself. The mansion was a constant meeting place for shipbuilders and foremen and Robert Stockton. Her own private rooms were taken over to make more space for her husband's work. Ericsson accused her of being "jealous of a steam engine." Without a quarrel, or even a cross word, Amelia returned to London. She had felt terribly out of place in the United States. She had felt uncomfortable in New York society. She had found the city crowded and dirty. She could not fit in. And, unlike her husband, she *could* accept defeat.

The *Princeton* was launched on September 7, 1843, with the words, "May it not bear the sword in vain, but be a terror to evildoers." The word *terror* did not apply as much to the sleek metal hull as it did to the 12-inch gun that was mounted on its deck. Ericsson's warship was complete. The drawings and the dream that he had carried with him from England four years earlier had taken shape and now floated before him. And Stockton had again gained Ericsson's trust and gratitude.

The feeling, at that moment, seemed mutual. Stockton's speech on Ericsson's behalf was clear. "I have searched the world over for a genius to invent a proper ship of war. He is my friend, here at my side." The words came more easily than the money that was owed Ericsson for his ship, and the credit for such a naval achievement was even less clear. The term "our ship" quickly became "my ship" in Stockton's words. Soon the *Princeton* became Robert Stockton's warship, and he even laid claim to the Oregon gun.

Stockton arranged a trial race between the *Princeton* and an English ship, the *Great Western,* to be held in New York harbor. The *Princeton* won the race easily, and two newspapers headlined the event as "The great Aquatic Race—Great Britain against America, and America against the world." Robert Stockton was proclaimed "the inventor of the marine marvel...the noble ship...the triumph in the art of naval defense." The real inventor stood quietly by, no doubt stunned and angry.

It was only when Stockton decided to replace the Oregon with a much larger and more powerful gun that Ericsson spoke up. "Stockton lacks sufficient knowledge for the planning of a common wheelbarrow...He never made a plan in his life." Ericsson knew that his gun was the right size to be carried by his ship. It was not so much the weight and the size of the Oregon that mattered. More important was the delicate balance. A larger gun would produce a large problem.

In a generous gesture to Ericsson, Stockton agreed not to replace the Oregon with the gun of his design. He would simply add his gun, the Peacemaker, to the ship. So the two great guns were carried on the bow and the stern of the *Princeton* as it glided down the Potomac in February 1844. There were also many government men aboard, and selected guests stood with Stockton at the center of the ship.

At the appropriate moment, Stockton announced the firing. His voice echoed among the guests and across the river. "Now, gentlemen, fellow citizens and shipmates, we are going to give a salute to the Mighty Republic. Stand firm and you will see how it feels!" There was a deafening blast, and the deck turned black with smoke. "It's nothing but honest gunpower, gentlemen; it has a strong smell of the Declaration of Independence," Stockton shouted above the crowd. The crowd was a little hesitant, but they were nonetheless impressed. They all agreed it was a great trip.

A few days later, Stockton arranged another party aboard the *Princeton*. The smoke had cleared and been forgotten. The excitement was well remembered. Five hundred even more distinguished guests were invited, including members of the cabinet, with their wives, and the president of the United States. Stockton promised an even greater voyage this time and an ever greater display of naval force. He would double the amount of gunpowder. John Ericsson was not aboard. Perhaps he knew what to expect and was wise enough to remain on land.

As they glided peacefully down the river, Stockton announced the firing of not one, but two guns. He proudly saluted his own gun, the Peacemaker, as a thunderous explosion of a 225-pound shell shattered the Peacemaker and ripped the *Princeton* apart. Many of the passengers and crew were killed or injured by the blast.

A reporter from the *Intelligencer* gave this record of the destruction:

> The imagination cannot picture to itself the half of the horrors. Wives widowed in an instant by the murderous blast! Daughters smitten with the heart-rending sight of their father's lifeless corpse! The wailing of agonized females; the grief of the unhurt by heart-stricken spectators! The wounded seamen borne down below. The silent and quivering lips of their own honest comrades who tried in vain to subdue or to conceal their feelings. What words can adequately depict a scene like this? The President escaped unhurt.

Although the ship was later repaired, the split between John Ericsson and Robert Stockton never was. Stockton blamed the entire incident on his "assistant, an ingenious mechanic, named Ericsson."

John Ericsson, who had wanted only to see his designs accepted, recognized the power of his invention to destroy. He had not meant to cause ruin. He had meant only to add to the nation's naval power. He had not yet thought of war, but war was to come. And John Ericsson's first warship, the *Princeton,* turned out to be the model for a ship used in the greatest naval battle of the Civil War.

10

A New American

"The people are much better than the travel books told me."

JOHN ERICSSON,
ON THE UNITED STATES

n the fall of 1846, Ericsson left his mansion and moved to the Union Club, where he found even more stimulating lodgers than those at the Astor House. He also found a style of living that was better suited to his bank balance, which was once again small. He sent Amelia a regular allowance that used up most of his income. He did not worry about that, however. In Ericsson's mind, living well meant being surrounded by interesting and capable people, exchanging ideas and plans. "Men, like engines, require food to keep up steam," he said.

The conversations at the Union Club centered on the increasing difference between the interest of the northern and southern States. The South would not give up its agricultural heritage, its system of slavery, and the plantation way of life. Southerners felt that the North, with its new industries, was sure to destroy the nation.

In those days, when discussions at the Union Club were not about politics, they might well have been about John Ericsson. He was well-liked and respected, and his company and views were in constant demand. He made friends with the noted Wall Street lawyer Edwin Wallace Stoughton and his wife, Mary. Ericsson cherished his privacy and usually did not allow women into his household, but Mary was always welcome. She came and went as she pleased, bringing her fascinating new friend flowers and food.

In America, Ericsson earned the warm affection of many individuals. When the Swedish singer Jenny Lind appeared in New York, she insisted on visiting her famous countryman and sang simple Swedish songs to please him. Fanny Kemble, a well-known Shakespearean actress, carried with her whenever she spoke a wooden lectern that Ericsson had designed and built for her.

But there were also those friends who had disappointed him. And although he had never been a person to hold a grudge, perhaps he forgot and forgave too quickly—at least in the case of his one-time sponsor, Robert Stockton. Ericsson was disturbed and angered by the treatment he had received from Stockton. He would not give in to defeat, however. His work always came first, so he hurried back to the Phoenix Foundry and to Delamater. He had one thing in mind. He would continue his search for a means of producing hot air power—the caloric engine.

His friend Cornelius Delamater wisely advised the impetuous Ericsson to stick to designing power engines and propellers. He told him it would take time to regain their navy's trust after the *Princeton* episode. He told him to wait on yet another revolutionary idea. "You know, John, that you can never convince a sailor."

Ericsson was impatient with having to wait, but he heeded Delamater's advice. Two years later, in 1846, Ericsson received a letter from the House Committee on Naval Affairs. Congress was interested in pursuing the idea of building an iron-hulled ship that was bullet proof. The congressman wanted detailed plans and designs.

Ericsson delivered them. He had put aside the *Princeton* design as being out-of-date—too thickly armored and too heavy. His new drawings were of a raft-like ship with engines beneath the water line. It would have guns mounted on circular rails, which could move and fire in any direction at any time.

Congress received the plans and put them aside. They looked too difficult to understand. Fifteen years later, Ericsson's design was taken from government files just in time to save the North from a Confederate attack, and aid in turning the tide of the Civil War.

Often frustrated, Ericsson did not stop trying to gain some sort of recognition for his ideas. When Congress set aside his plans for a warship, he returned to the study of natural resources that had fascinated him as a child. He developed steam-pumping engines that could force water up as high as four stories. There the water would be stored in large roof tanks. Then, by the force of gravity, the water would flow down and supply the floors below.

Such inventions did interest Ericsson, but by now he had progressed far beyond them. He had entered the world of warships.

In was a world with a long and profuse history, dating back to about 3300 B.C. when the Iron Age in Greece began. From those early times down to the 19th century, wind and oar power had been the only means of propelling a warship. There had been thousands of changes in fire power and rigging, and the size of naval vessels had grown from around 65 feet to more than 300 feet. But little had been done about "driving" the warship. It was still at the mercy of the wind and the strength of men to move it. It was not until Ericsson's day that naval warfare experienced a revolution. The changes first took place in the United States amid the prosperity of the late 1840s, and the inventors and engineers were fast at work.

The wealth of the United States was particularly evident in New York City. Although many men had hurried west in the gold rush, the East still controlled finance. Also, the major banks were located in New York City.

Ericsson, surrounded by men of wealth and power, often forgot that he was just an inventor, always in search of a buyer for his ideas. Also, on occasion he still forgot to apply for his patents and would frequently find that his inventions were being registered in someone else's name. He was still failing to get much of the recognition and financial rewards he deserved. Moreover, whenever he did receive a substantial sum of money, he sent a generous amount to Amelia.

John Ericsson, whose love of invention was marred by a lack of good business sense.

Ericsson began the year 1850 with a bank balance of $132.32, a rather large amount in those days. He turned his bank balance and creative energies to an old idea he had played with back in Sweden. Water heated to the boiling point produced steam, and steam could move anything. He had proved that. What if you heated air to high temperatures? Would hot air move anything? Could hot air produce the same results as steam? And at less cost? He had more questions, and more questions led to answers. He started his experiments in the use of hot air.

Then in 1851, he was invited to display some of his accomplishments at London's Crystal Palace exposition. He submitted devices for measuring distances at sea, for measuring fluids, for indicating high temperatures, and for determining ocean depths. It must have given Ericsson great pleasure and satisfaction finally to gain recognition from England, the country that had previously ignored his achievements. Queen Victoria described the exposition, which displayed products from all over the world, as "extraordinary, but beyond my powers to attempt to explain." Ericsson described the exposition as a "tremendous advance in international cooperation and in the spread of knowledge of the arts and sciences."

Despite this sudden recognition, Ericsson was happy to be in America, rather than England. He wrote to a friend in Sweden, "I am very well satisfied with America. The people are much better than the travel books told me. I never felt better."

Three years earlier, in October of 1848, Ericsson had become a United States citizen. Of all the awards he received later in his life, that single piece of paper that made him a citizen was the one that he prized the most.

THE ERICSSON

"Ericsson is the great mechanical genius of the
present and the future."

The New York Tribune

John Ericsson's adopted country was a land of many
nationalities. The United States had at its disposal the
knowledge and culture of many lands. People had the
freedom to develop themselves to their full potential. In this
atmosphere, Ericsson was able to search for answers to his never-
ending questions and to watch and wait for new opportunities.

He did not have to wait long. In the July 1852 issue of *Merchant's
Magazine,* a writer stated that "the age is ripe for change. A new
motive power is demanded and if the eyesight and judgment can be
relied upon, it has appeared. It is the most sublime development of
force ever seen in machinery." He was talking about the caloric
engine.

Ericsson had spent most of his career working on the use of heat
as a mechanical force. Ten years before, he had built several caloric
engines, small ones at first, then gradually larger and larger ones.
All the time, he aimed at saving fuel. How could he do this? How
could he reuse heated air from the exhaust mechanism along with
fresh air? He found the answer in a cylinder that could transfer the
heated exhaust air to the compressed air in the working cylinder of

the engine. This transfer of heat from the air going out to the air coming in took place in a wire-meshed box that he called the regenerator. Then, for additional heat, he placed a small fire box below the working cylinder. The result was a hot-air engine, which operated more simply and with greater efficiency than any steam engine ever could. It was the forerunner of the gas turbine that followed many, many years later, when airplanes began to cross the skies.

Now it remained for Ericsson to combine his two great conceptions into a single design. He built the first caloric ship and called it the *Ericsson*. It must have given him great satisfaction at last to have his own name on one of his inventions.

The *Ericsson* was a large steamship with caloric engines operating its paddlewheels. The two connected cylinders generated the power to move the pistons. With the use of the regenerator, the engine could run for three hours without the need for more fuel. A steam engine paled in comparison. But the threat of "this new thing" bothered businessmen who had tied up their money in steam. Ericsson had once again run into his old obstacle—the hesitation of established society to accept new ideas. However, the recent explosion of several steam vessels convinced the owner of a southern steamship line, Gazaway Bugg Lamar, to put a great deal of money into Ericsson's new engine. Lamar was especially concerned because he had just lost his wife and six children in a steamboat explosion off the Carolina coast.

From the moment the *Ericsson* keel was laid in April 1852, the publicity and anticipation were high. The *London Daily News* printed a letter:

> To that part of the public who travel, to those who send merchandise from one end of the world to another, to all those who contribute large subsidies to steam companies that have no interest in selling coal or building steam engines . . . the caloric ship will be all gain and no loss. As sure as water will find its level, the use of the caloric engine will force its way.

More people invested money in the ship. The rich people wanted to become richer, and poorer people wanted to become rich. Immigrants no longer wanted to watch things happen. They wanted to make things happen, too. They cried out for political change, labor equality, and social reform. They, too, wanted to become capitalists, to grab at new ideas and speculations. They welcomed the first steam-driven balloon and the first hot-air ship. The sky was indeed the limit.

The *Ericsson* was launched in September 1852 and was called a luxury liner. It was 260 feet long with a 40-foot beam. Half of the $500,000 it cost to build the ship was spent on the engines alone. Newspapers reported that "[no] ship sailing out of this port will surpass the *Ericsson* in beauty and completeness of interior appointments." Ericsson read this report with little interest. The ship had been built as a luxury liner because the sponsors had insisted upon it. They had wanted the inside to be lavish and elegant.

The inventor had simply wanted the mechanical parts of the *Ericsson* to work well. Therefore, the words of two articles praising the technology of the ship meant much more to him than most printed reports. "We have never seen anything to compare with the castings," the *Scientific American* article read. "Captain Ericsson is a very skillful, scientific and ingenious engineer." And the *New York Tribune* said: "Ericsson is the great mechanical genius of the present and the future. The age of steam is closed. The age of caloric opens."

Ericsson had certainly stirred up the people and the press. The following month, February, he received word that he had stirred up the United States Congress as well. The secretary of the navy sent a letter to the House Committee on Naval Affairs. It read:

For the consideration of Congress, this vessel presents the first exhibition of the application of the new caloric engine invented by Captain Ericsson, a gentleman whose genius has enabled him to secure to the naval and mercantile marine of our country the most valuable auxiliary power in the navigation of ships that has yet been furnished to the world—a power which is destined hereafter to become of universal application in the driving of machinery, whether on land or sea.... I respectfully submit to Congress... the passage of a resolution to direct the Secretary of the Navy forthwith to make a contract with Captain Ericsson for the construction, under the superintendent of the Department, of one Ericsson frigate of not less than 2,000 tons, to be equipped with caloric engines of sufficient power, as a ship of war.

Ericsson was flattered and very much tempted by the proposal. However—possibly for the first time in his life—he was hesitant. He knew that his caloric engines could produce a maximum speed of only 12 revolutions per minute. He could not, in all honesty and safety, force them faster. He knew they would surely fail when pushed to the high speeds required by a battleship.

Orson Munn, part owner of the *Scientific American,* wrote in that magazine that

one day recently the wheels of this ship moved and straightway every daily paper in our city noticed the important event. When they touch upon scientific matters, they utter the most consummate nonsense. Here is the substance of the language used by them all. "Fire was applied to the furnaces for the first time yesterday and resulted in the triumphant success of the experiment. At the start the wheels made 3 turns per minute. This is much more than the friends of the invention had reason to expect." Those who reported the event must have been a long time headed up in barrels... If the moving of the wheels of the "caloric ship" is much more than the ardent friends of the invention had reason to expect, why in the name of common sense did they build it?

Ericsson's sponsors did not share his reluctance to build the caloric battleship. But Congress, at the last minute, did listen to him. What could have resulted in yet another naval disaster fortunately was prevented. That particular ship was not built.

However, the Congress had given Ericsson another question to answer. Could he build a battleship using both his propeller and his caloric engine? During the following year, he worked endlessly to answer the question. After making many drawings and trying many experiments, he discovered that cast iron could not stand the high temperature necessary to work the caloric engine. The regenerator was effective with smaller engines, but it could not help an iron-hulled battleship. He firmly believed that "this extraordinary system of obtaining motive power" could "some day be perfected," but not now. It was not practical. He would have to study it further, and since Congress was now thinking about war, Ericsson returned to thinking about steam.

On the evening of April 27, 1854, he and a few guests were cruising in New York harbor aboard the *Ericsson*. It was a special event for the inventor to be aboard his beautiful caloric ship, which seemed destined to be just a pleasure craft. Suddenly, a squall came up, and fierce winds and rain sank the *Ericsson*. He and his friends were saved—just in time to watch from small boats as the "mechanical marvel" disappeared beneath the water.

A few days later, the *Ericsson* was raised. Then, in order to cut costs, it was equipped with steam. The newspapers reported that "the epoch-making caloric ship was indeed among the things that were."

This report, combined with his pride and his 20 years of dedication, led Ericsson once again to devote himself to the caloric engine. He would meet the challenge. He was his old self again, determined to refuse defeat. He applied his caloric engine to printing presses, water pumps, pleasure yachts, lighthouses, sewing machines, and anything else that called for a "limited, economical, safe and self-managed motor." It was in great demand for any and all small enterprises. Ericsson wrote to a friend "that the engines have been running constantly and that they are in the most perfect order." He felt confident that now his caloric engine was perfected and ready for a large enterprise.

On August 29, 1861, Ericsson wrote a letter to President Abraham Lincoln. "I seek no private advantage or emolument [payment] of any kind. Fortunately, I have upward of one thousand of my caloric engines in successful operation with affluence in prospect." He proposed to build an iron battleship that would use caloric power.

President Lincoln did not refuse. Four months before, on April 12, 1861, the Civil War had started.

THE CIVIL WAR

"A house divided against itself cannot stand."
ABRAHAM LINCOLN

The Civil War came as no surprise. Conflicting values had existed within the United States for 40 years. The Missouri compromise of 1820 dealt with the question of the expansion of slavery. It stated that there would be an equal number of slave states and free states admitted to the Union within certain boundaries. However, as territories increased, conflicts arose. Opinions clashed at the admission of each state. Slaves were classified as property, and Southern slaveowners felt that they had a constitutional right to take their property to any part of the Union.

Northerners did not agree. The Northern states hired free people, people who had come as immigrants to the United States. The influx of new immigrants, and the fact that Northerners by and large stayed in the North, increased the population of the Northern states. The North expanded its railroads, linking new "Midwest" states to the North and East. The North harnessed industry and began to build a strong economy. This left the Southern states in a different situation. The South, however, resisted changing its agricultural way of life to copy the industrial North. Stephen Foster wrote songs praising the proud and happy

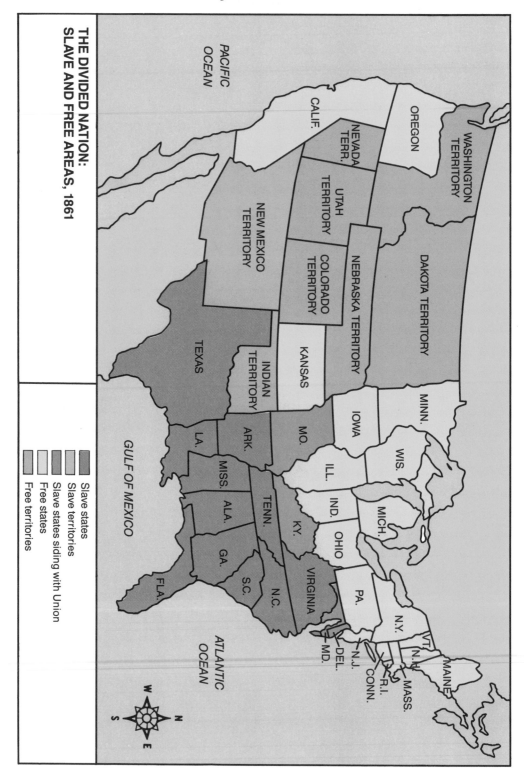

THE DIVIDED NATION:
SLAVE AND FREE AREAS, 1861

Slave states
Slave territories
Slave states siding with Union
Free states
Free territories

way of life in the land of cotton. Meanwhile, in the North, Abraham Lincoln proclaimed, "A house divided against itself cannot stand."

The South, which had $2 billion invested in slaves, viewed slavery as an economic necessity. In the North, however, slavery was seen as a moral issue. "Abolish slavery," a group of Northerners insisted, but the South ignored the cry and held on to its slaves. The Southerners pointed to the glory of ancient civilizations in which slavery had been praised. They quoted from the Bible, attempting to demonstrate that God had indeed created inferior races. They argued that they took better care of their slave workers than Northerners took of wage earners.

The Northerners pointed to the Declaration of Independence, which says that all men are created equal.

In 1831, William Lloyd Garrison founded an antislavery newspaper, declaring: "On this subject I do not wish to think, or speak, or write, with moderation. . . . I will be harsh as truth and as uncompromising as justice. . . . I am in earnest—I will not equivocate—I will not excuse—I will not retreat a single inch. AND I WILL BE HEARD." He was heard loud and clear as the movement to end slavery grew stronger and stronger in the North. Southerners, on the other hand, dreamed of spreading their beliefs across the nation, and subduing the North.

The roar on the floor of Congress equaled the roar of guns that was to follow. As new states were added to the Union, new representatives took the North's side. The South was outnumbered and more and more ready to fight. Then in 1849, when California requested admission into the Union with a constitution prohibiting slavery, the South talked openly of leaving the Union to form a separate nation—so began the move toward secession.

This led to long and heated debates in the Senate. Henry Clay spoke against prohibiting slavery in the new territories. He told the South that secession was unconstitutional and that further talk of it would not be tolerated. Then Senator James Mason of Virginia spoke: "I have, Senators, believed from the first that the agitation on the subject of slavery would, if not prevented by some timely and effective measure, end in disunion." His friend Henry Clay added with booming emphasis, "The North must cease the agitation of the slave question."

Daniel Webster answered him. "I wish to speak today not as a Massachusetts man, not as a Northern man, but as an American. I speak today for the preservation of the Union." Then he clearly warned the South that secession was out of the question. "Sir, your eyes and mine are never destined to see that miracle! . . . There can be no such thing as a peaceable secession."

On June 13, 1858, Abraham Lincoln became the Republican candidate for the Senate from Illinois. His acceptance speech was filled with references to the slavery issue and the threat of secession.

> I believe this government cannot endure permanently half slave and half free. I do not expect the Union to be dissolved. I do not expect the house to fall, but I do expect it will cease to be divided. It will become all one thing or all the other. Either the opponents of slavery will arrest the further spread of it and place it where the public mind shall rest in the belief that it is in the course of ultimate extinction; or its advocates will push it forward until it shall become alike lawful in all the States, old as well as new, North as well as South.

Lincoln's Democratic opponent was Stephen Douglas. Both their campaigns for the Senate hinged on the issue of slavery. They argued back and forth across the nation in the now-famous Lincoln-Douglas debates. Lincoln lost the senatorial election, but less than two years later he was put forth as the Republican candidate for president. He won the election of 1860. A few months later, in an inspiring inaugural address on March 4, 1861, he warned the South:

> Suppose you go to war, you cannot fight always; and when, after much loss on both sides and no gain on either, you cease fighting, the identical old questions as to terms of intercourse [discussion] are again upon you. In your hands, my dissatisfied fellow country men, and not in mine, is the momentous issue of civil war. The government will not assail you. You have no oath registered in

heaven to destroy the government, while I shall have the most solemn one to preserve, protect, defend it. We are not enemies, but friends.

Lincoln's speech made sense to many, but it did not satisfy the Southerners, who wanted more than ever to form a union of their own. They believed Lincoln to be strictly opposed to slavery, and they saw his election as a definite threat to them. So the move toward secession continued. As far west as California, there was talk of separating and of creating "a new Pacific nation."

In 1861, 11 Southern states left the Union and formed the Confederate States of America. Daniel Webster's eloquent words of more than 20 years before—"Liberty and Union, now and forever, one and inseparable!"—rang hollow now. The United States was divided, crumbling over the matter of states' rights.

The citizens of the Southern states, led by their president, Jefferson Davis, rose 10 million strong to subdue the Northern states, whose population was 22 million. The men of the North joined forces to fight the threat of the South.

As President Lincoln said:

If the two sections can no longer live together, they can no longer live apart in quiet till it is determined which is master. No two civilizations ever did, or can, come into contact as the North and South threaten to do, without a trial of strength, in which the weaker goes to the wall. . . . We must remain master of the occasion and the dominant power on this continent.

President Lincoln had tried his best to control the problem with logic and persuasion, but talk had not worked. It was time for action now. After much thought, he decided that the best way to handle the situation was to wait for an aggressive act by the South. The North could encourage such action by sending additional troops and supplies to Fort Sumter, one of the four Union-held forts in Confederate territory. A few days later, Charleston, South

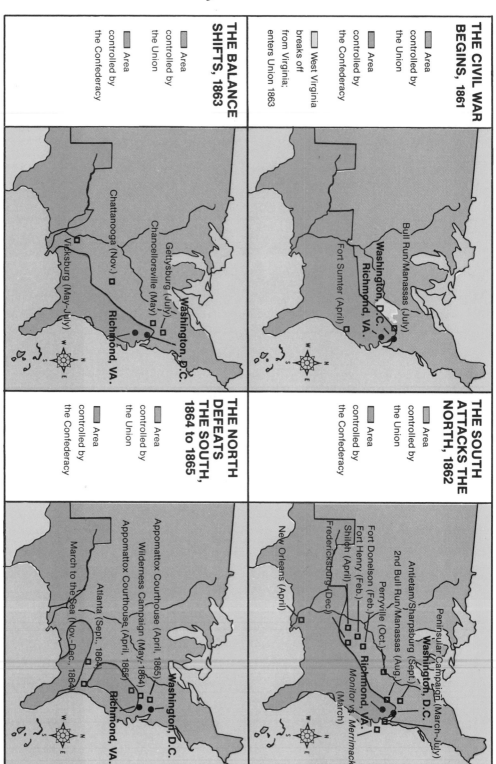

THE CIVIL WAR BEGINS, 1861

☐ Area controlled by the Union

▨ Area controlled by the Confederacy

☐ West Virginia breaks off from Virginia; enters Union 1863

THE BALANCE SHIFTS, 1863

☐ Area controlled by the Union

▨ Area controlled by the Confederacy

Vicksburg (May–July)
Chattanooga (Nov.)
Gettysburg (July)
Chancellorsville (May)
Washington, D.C.
Richmond, VA.

THE SOUTH ATTACKS THE NORTH, 1862

☐ Area controlled by the Union

▨ Area controlled by the Confederacy

Bull Run/Manassas (July)
Fort Sumter (April)
Washington, D.C.
Richmond, VA.

THE NORTH DEFEATS THE SOUTH, 1864 to 1865

☐ Area controlled by the Union

▨ Area controlled by the Confederacy

Appomattox Courthouse (April, 1865)
Wilderness Campaign (May, 1864)
Appomattox Courthouse (April, 1865)
Atlanta (Sept. 1864)
March to the Sea (Nov.–Dec., 1864)
Washington, D.C.
Richmond, VA.

New Orleans (April)
Antietam/Sharpsburg (Sept.)
2nd Bull Run/Manassas (Aug.)
Perryville (Oct.)
Fort Donelson (Feb.)
Fort Henry (Feb.)
Shiloh (April)
Fredericksburg (Dec.)
Peninsular Campaign (March–July)
Washington, D.C.
Richmond, VA.
Monitor vs. Merrimack (March)

A Union flag bearer. The Civil War was the most bitter and costly war the United States had ever known.

Carolina, echoed with the first cannon-blasts of battle—prelude to a war that would last four long years.

In September 1862, with the Civil War well underway, President Lincoln issued the Emancipation Proclamation. This document declared that on January 1, 1863, all Southern slaves would be "then, henceforward and forever free." The war became still more fierce. "The Bonnie Blue Flag," the anthem of the Confederacy, was played on trumpet, fife, and drum. The "Battle Hymn of the Republic" was the anthem of the Union troops. The gray uniformed Southerners met the blue-clad Northerners in hand-to-hand combat, while the roar of cannons and the crack of rifles shattered the air.

The Civil War was a personal war in many ways. It was a war of emotions. The political problems centered on the exploding economic competition between North and South. The social problems centered on the views of a slower-paced and agricultural Southern life in contrast to a more industrial Northern life. The North had many powerful cities and a strong economy. The South had an agricultural heritage and a strong belief in its way of life.

THE MONITOR AND THE MERRIMACK

"A tin can on a raft."

A CONFEDERATE SOLDIER'S
DESCRIPTION OF THE MONITOR

he Union navy was faced with a definite crisis. Its ships were all wooden-hulled. The enemy was hard at work. Fourteen hundred men were busy at the Gosport Shipyard and the Tredegar Iron Works in Richmond, Virginia. They were busy turning out battleships reinforced with iron hulls. The idea of iron plating was not new. It dated back to medieval times, when warriors held shields against attack. The idea of applying iron plating to battleships was new, however. In 1854, ironclads, or warships with iron plates, were used by France and Britain against Russia in the Crimean War. During the two years of that war, these iron-hulled ships had proved very effective. France was the first country to use them, and Britain followed closely behind, after realizing the value of a hull that no gun could shoot through.

John Ericsson had offered his plans for an armored ship to France before that war. France had turned down the design as "an amusing experiment," just as England had turned down the Ericsson screw propeller.

Now the inventor's proposal to President Lincoln for an "iron battleship equipped with caloric power" came at a most appropriate time. On April 12, 1861, Confederate troops fired the first shots of the war on Fort Sumter, a fort in Charleston, South Carolina. One week later, the president ordered a naval blockade of the Confederate coastline. A blockade—the blocking of an area by military means—would mean that the Confederates would not be able to enter or leave their territory by sea. But there were not enough Union ships to accomplish this.

The Civil War gave Ericsson, a man of peace, his greatest opportunity. But the opportunity did not come easily or quickly. It came, rather, by accident. Congress debated long and hard in heated sessions concerning the value of iron-hulled vessels. The talks centered on one ship in particular. The *Merrimack* was the newest of the United States steamships. It would be extremely important for the defense of either side, and it was at the Gosport Shipyard. So the Union navy's newly appointed engineer in chief, Benjamin Franklin Isherwood, persuaded navy secretary Gideon Welles to let him go to the shipyard and lay claim to the *Merrimack* for the Union. He was well aware that if the North secured it, the South would be at a great disadvantage.

When Isherwood arrived at the shipyard, however, he found that nothing had been done to prepare the great ship for war. Its engines were scattered about in the yard's workshops.

Commodore Charles S. McCauley was in command at Gosport. He was a Northerner, an aging naval officer who had long ago lost his enthusiasm for active duty. He had been assigned to what he thought to be a comfortable and safe haven. He was happy to sit around and do nothing but watch the big ships come and go. When an order came in for a ship delivery, he spoke to his staff about it and, in due time, the job was done. There were 12 Southerners on his staff, yet he never questioned their motives when they assured him that the *Merrimack* could be made ready for war within one month's time.

Isherwood did not agree. He knew it would take much longer, and time was running out. Virginia was seceding from the Union, and anti-Union feelings were strong in Portsmouth and Norfolk. Isherwood feared that any day the rebellion would spill over into the yard, and angry Virginians would seize the ships. He immediately told McCauley to order three crews to work around the clock and get the *Merrimack* in shape for battle, but McCauley refused. Isherwood later described the Commodore at the time:

> He sat in his office, immovable, not knowing what to do.... He listened blandly, or seemed to listen, to what was said to him, but could not be made to give any order or take any action.... I endeavored to...make him understand the necessity of getting the *Merrimack* out at once, and I told him we could tow out at the same time several other vessels. I knew the Navy Yard would be in our possession but a few days longer, and wanted to save all the public property that I could, as well as to diminish the force of the enemy by preventing it from falling into their hands. All was in vain.

Finally, Isherwood gave a preliminary order himself to at least recondition the ship, the *Merrimack*'s engines in place, get its boilers fired and ready, and replace its cable chains with rope that could be more easily cut to set her free to sail the minute McCauley gave the order. The tide was running out, and time was short. But McCauley never gave the order. He told Isherwood that he had decided to defend the yard instead. "I looked at him with amazement," Isherwood said.

> I went over the case again, urged the orders...upon him, told him the inevitable consequences of his decision, tried to show him the utter absurdity of attempting to defend an unfortified navy yard without men or any military means at command, for by this time he was absolutely alone. Finding that I could not move him and that he was growing impatient at my reiterated appeals, I drew from my pocket the order of the Department to me, wrote upon it the usual endorsement that, having completed the duty assigned to me I was to return to Washington. He signed without a word.... As I witnessed the gradual dying out of the revolutions of the Merrimack's engines at the dock, I was tempted to cut the ropes that held her and bring her out on my own responsibility.

So the *Merrimack* was lost to the North. The South could thank the enemy for delivering into its hands its most valuable naval gift. Almost immediately, Stephen Mallory, the secretary of the Confederate navy, acted with decision. He sent a letter to the Norfolk Navy Yard: "You will proceed with all practical dispatch to make changes in the *Merrimack* and to build, equip, and fit her in all respects." The Confederate government renamed the ship the *Virginia,* though it was (and is) still commonly known as the *Merrimack.*

Meanwhile, John Ericsson's proposal letter to the president had not been answered, and neither had his follow-up letter to the Ironclad Board. This board was a group of men who had been appointed by the secretary of the navy to direct naval warfare. In time of war, the mail bags bulged with countless letters to the president. They were from everyone and everywhere, expressing ideas, promises, and anger. Most of them ended up in the White House wastebasket. Perhaps this is what happened to John Ericsson's letter.

Finally, Cornelius Delamater took the matter in hand. He went to Washington on "business" for his iron works. There he ran into his good friend Cornelius Bushnell, who was a staunch supporter of the Union and a strong advocate of the iron-hulled ship. He was also a close friend of Gideon Welles, the secretary of the navy. After the two men had discussed the Union's problem for a short time, Delamater advised his friend "to consult the engineer John Ericsson at New York, as one whose opinion would settle the matter definitely and with accuracy."

Immediately, Bushnell took a train to New York, talked with Ericsson, and returned the next day with a model for the *Monitor.* He showed the raft-like toy ship to Welles, who looked at it with approval, and to President Lincoln. At this point, in desperation, the navy had been mounting guns on every available thing that could float. Why not try a raft? The raft was a low, flat boat. It was an ingenious idea, because a ship with a flat bottom could float in shallow water.

The Ironclad Board did not agree. The board remembered John Ericsson and the *Princeton*. They told Bushnell to "take the model home. It is the image of nothing in the heavens above, or in the earth beneath, or in the waters under the earth."

Bushnell did not go home. Instead he went back to New York and persuaded Ericsson to go back to Washington with him. He did not tell the inventor about his own failed attempt before the board. He merely said that "Secretary Welles wishes you to come right on and make your explanations before the entire board in his room at the department."

Ericsson went, but as he talked he sensed the hostility in the room. The answer to his proposal was a hesitant "no." But his persistent character and his habit of questioning everything forced him to ask just one question more. "Why?" There was a long silence and no answer, so he continued with a vivid speech, listing the "stability, maneuverability, invulnerability of his ship's fighting qualities, its relatively low cost... and its promised time of delivery: 100 days." He reminded his listeners of the Southern ship which was ready and waiting. The *Virginia* was a very strong foe. Then he ended his speech with a direct demand. "I consider it your duty to your country to give me an order to build the vessel before I leave this room." The order was given.

Ericsson left at once for New York with only a verbal commitment. He produced his *Monitor* in the promised 100 days.

The flat-bottomed *Monitor* was 172 feet long and weighed 776 tons, complete with armor plating from five to eight inches thick. In the center of its deck was a revolving armored turret, or gun mount. It was 20 feet in diameter and held two heavy Dahlgren cannons. They were reinforced with thick iron bands to withstand strong firing charges. The guns were mounted side by side. Until this time, a vessel had to turn broadside to fire at the enemy. This was a long, slow process. The *Monitor's* turret was a revolutionary change. It could turn and fire on the enemy from any direction.

The ship cleared the water by only three feet. The hidden screw propeller and steam engines enabled the ship to travel with speed and ease.

On February 17, 1862, the C.S.S. *Virginia,* more widely known as the *Merrimack,* was commissioned by the Confederate navy, and it steamed out of Norfolk. On February 25, the *Monitor,* informally referred to as the "tin can," steamed out of New York. Both ships were headed for Hampton Roads in Virginia, the dividing water line between North and South. President Lincoln had ordered the navy to set up a blockade to protect Washington, the capital of the Union. There were more than 60 ships in the area—ships of all sizes and types from transport vessels to small tugboats and ferries. But the *Merrimack* and the *Monitor* were the two ships that would engage in one of the most historic naval battles of the Civil War.

The *Merrimack* was 262 feet, 9 inches long and was reinforced with four inches of thick armor. The ship carried 10 assorted guns—four rifles and six smaller Dahlgren cannons. Its mission was to clear Hampton Roads of every Union ship. On March 8, it did its duty well, performing before an audience of men, women, and children from the Confederate Fort Monroe. They had all

Crewmen on the U.S.S. *Monitor*, drilling with a field gun. This gun was not used in the combat at Hampton Roads.

rushed down to the river-bank to witness the battle. They proudly proclaimed that "as soon as the *Merrimack* rammed a vessel, she would sink her with all hands enclosed in an iron-plated coffin." They were right. The *Merrimack* rammed and sank the *Cumberland*, a sailing ship carrying 24 guns. Pilot Smith of the doomed ship observed that they did not stand a chance against the ironclad *Merrimack*. "Volleys bounced off her like India-rubber balls."

Then the dreaded ship turned around and attacked the *Congress*, which carried 47 guns. The *Congress* became a blazing bonfire. When the *Merrimack* faced the *Minnesota*, the *Minnesota* turned and ran aground. The *Merrimack* was a true conqueror. The naval blockade was burning and sinking fast in the wake of this iron battleship. The day had been victorious for the Confederate side. Two hundred and fifty Union people were instantly killed and many more were wounded. On the Confederate side, only 60 people had been lost. The Union was in a panic. There was no doubt that the next day the *Merrimack* would finish the job. The blockade would be broken and the capital no longer protected.

That night, however, the *Monitor* arrived. It was almost invisible in the darkness as it slid next to the *Roanoke* and dropped anchor. When Commanding Officer Worden heard of the death and destruction on the waters that day, he "vowed vengeance" on the *Merrimack*. And when he heard of the forced grounding of the *Minnesota,* he knew that the Confederate ship would be back in the morning to finish it off. He knew what had to be done. "The *Merrimack* has caused sad work amongst our vessels, but she can't hurt us," he stated with confidence. And he made straight toward the *Minnesota* to rescue it.

When the *Minnesota's* chief engineer gave the word that the *Monitor* was alongside, "a cheer went up that might have been heard in Richmond."

Back in Washington, there was much noise and confusion. The *Merrimack* had to be stopped. At any moment, even President Lincoln expected to see the "Rebel Monster" steaming up the Potomac River. Messages were sent to the governors of New York, Massachusetts, and Maine, advising them "to defend their ports with heavy batteries and large timber rafts to obstruct the ironclad's passage." It was also suggested that large barges be sunk in the Potomac in order to stop the *Merrimack's* advance on the capital.

The newspapers blamed the whole disaster on Hampton Roads "on the terrible evidence of how active and daring are the rebels, and how sleepy, slow, and self-satisfied are we."

Thinking back to Gosport Shipyard, Benjamin Franklin Isherwood must have heartily agreed.

A New Yorker remarked sadly, "What next? Why should not this invulnerable marine demon breach the walls of Fortress Monroe, raise the blockade, and destroy New York and Boston?"

John Ericsson had the answer, and it had already arrived at Hampton Roads.

THE BATTLE

"We never got sight of her guns except when they were about to fire into us."

LT. JOHN EGGLESTON,
ABOARD THE MONITOR

efore dawn on March 9, the sailors on the *Merrimack* awakened to the sounds of fife and drum. They rushed topside to peer through the early morning fog. In the distance, they saw the *Minnesota,* still aground. That would be their first target today, and today the Union naval blockade would surely be destroyed. The Confederates could see a great victory. What they could not see was the *Monitor,* hidden under the *Minnesota's* bow.

Aboard the *Monitor* the men cleaned up the ship, loaded their guns, and waited for the *Merrimack* to try and make the kill. They had not slept that night in fear that when the tide returned, the badly crippled *Minnesota* might come free and bear down on them. They had spent the night moving back and forth in the dark channel.

As dawn appeared, tugs and barges surrounded the helpless ship, trying in every way to get it afloat. Paymaster Keeler on the *Monitor* watched as "bags and hammocks of the men and barrels and bags of provisions... went into the boats and some into the water, which was covered with barrels of rice, whiskey, flour, beans, sugar... thrown overboard to lighten the ship.

William Rogers, at Fort Monroe, sadly watched the heroic efforts to haul the huge ship off the mud banks. It "seemed to be doomed to destruction" like its "companions of the previous day." He also watched members of the crews for the sunken ships, the *Cumberland* and the *Congress,* as they tramped, wounded and bloody, from Newport News, a Union port, back to the Fort.

It was believed that the South was advancing on Newport News. General Wool did not think that a large Confederate cavalry division had been brought up just to witness the *Merrimack's* operations. In desperation he had dispatched a telegram to General McClellan:

I want for immediate defense, to be sent as soon as possible, 2,000 regular infantry and 8,000 volunteer infantry; five batteries of light artillery, regulars if possible; 1,100 horses to furnish the five batteries, to complete the batteries I have here, and for the unmounted cavalry. The rebels are threatening Newport News. Scouts report they have appeared in large force within five miles of that port. With this force I can evacuate Newport News by land if necessary. You can probably best determine, from a knowledge of the enemy's movements near you, what additional force I may require. I want three quartermasters, the chief of whom should be a superior man, and four brigadier-generals, with an efficient staff.

Brigadier-General Joseph Mansfield—commander of the Union troops at Newport News—did not share General Wool's panicked concern. He thought that the rebels had come just to witness a great naval battle. If indeed that was their thought, they were certainly not alone in it.

Once again, the banks along the river were filling with eager spectators, who were waiting for the fight. They juggled back and forth for the best "seats," like ticket holders for a boxing match. Then they caught sight of the *Monitor.*

Lieutenant Rochelle, who was aboard the Confederate ship *Patrick Henry,* probably expressed the surprise of all the spectators when he observed that

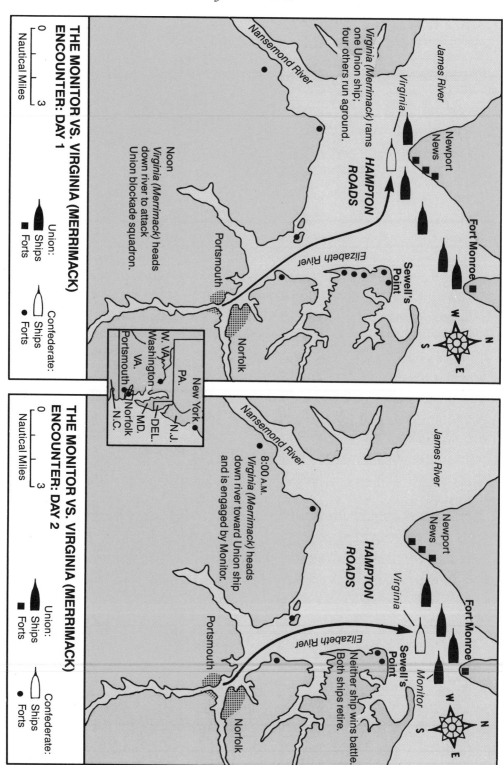

**THE MONITOR VS. VIRGINIA (MERRIMACK)
ENCOUNTER: DAY 1**

0   3
Nautical Miles

Union:
▲ Ships
■ Forts

Confederate:
⬯ Ships
● Forts

Virginia (Merrimack) rams
one Union ship;
four others run aground.

Noon
Virginia (Merrimack) heads
down river to attack
Union blockade squadron.

Nansemond River

Virginia

HAMPTON
ROADS

Newport
News

James River

Fort Monroe

Sewell's
Point

Elizabeth River

Portsmouth

Norfolk

N
W   E
S

PA.
W. VA.
Washington
VA.
Portsmouth
Norfolk
N.C.
MD.
DEL.
N.J.
New York

**THE MONITOR VS. VIRGINIA (MERRIMACK)
ENCOUNTER: DAY 2**

0   3
Nautical Miles

Union:
▲ Ships
■ Forts

Confederate:
⬯ Ships
● Forts

8:00 A.M.
Virginia (Merrimack) heads
down river toward Union ship
and is engaged by Monitor.

Nansemond River

Virginia

HAMPTON
ROADS

Newport
News

James River

Fort Monroe

Monitor

Sewell's
Point

Both ships retire.
Neither ship wins battle.

Elizabeth River

Portsmouth

Norfolk

N
W   E
S

The U.S.S. *Minnesota* deliberately ran itself aground rather than face fire from the *Merrimack.*

the *Minnesota* was discovered in her old position but the *Minnesota* was not the only thing to attract attention. Close alongside of her lay such a craft as the eyes of a seaman never looked upon before— an immense shingle floating on the water, with a gigantic cheese-box rising from its center; no sails, no wheels, no smokestack, no guns. What could it be? On board the *Patrick Henry* many were the surmises as to the strange craft. Some thought it a water tank sent to supply the *Minnesota* with water; others were of opinion that it was a floating magazine replenishing her exhausted stock of ammunition; a few visionary characters feebly intimated that it might be the *Monitor* which the Northern papers had been boasting about for a long time.

The *Merrimack* steamed full speed ahead toward the hopelessly injured and helpless *Minnesota.* The *Merrimack's* guns were ready to destroy her. Suddenly, as the fog lifted, the pilot spotted "an iron battery near her." He called to the commanding officer, who commented that it was "the strangest craft he had ever seen before." He decided that it was a raft for rescuing doomed crew. The soldiers dubbed it a "cheese box on a raft." And the *Baltimore American* correspondent wrote that at best it was "the reverse of formidable."

The crew aboard the *Minnesota* was busy preparing for its fate. They had less than an hour to strip the ship of guns so the enemy would not take them. Most of the crew's personal belongings were already gone, either into the surrounding tug boats or into the water. But the guns were of major concern, and there was not much time left. The *Merrimack* was bearing down. In the midst of the panic and confusion, the *Monitor* raised her anchor and steamed ahead. But as one of its crew said, "To tell the truth, we did not have much faith in the *Monitor.* The *Monitor* was so small. The *Virginia* was so big."

The *Monitor* crew waited inside the buttoned-up hatch for the order to fire. There is some confusion as to which ship fired the first shot. However, Keeler on board the *Monitor* saw a puff of smoke rising above the *Merrimack* as a "shell howled over our heads and crashed into the side of the *Minnesota.* Captain Worden ordered the *Monitor's* crew below. Then he pointed to the twin gun muzzles which were being loaded with shot weighing 180 pounds, and told his gunners to 'send them with our compliments.'"

Captain Van Brunt, standing on the deck of the *Minnesota,* observed how the *Monitor* "immediately ran down in my wake, right within range of the *Merrimack,* completely covering my ship as far as was possible with her dimensions, and, much to my astonishment, laid herself right alongside of the *Virginia* and the contrast was that of a pygmy to a giant."

When the *Monitor* fired its first shot, the crew of 350 men on the *Merrimack* did not believe it. They thought that the boiler on the strange vessel had blown up. The *Merrimack* continued toward its target. "We never got sight of her guns except when they were about to fire into us," L. John Eggleston declared. The guns would fire, and the revolving turret would then turn them out of sight. For the men on the *Merrimack,* it was like fighting blind. The big ship was being splintered by an almost invisible dwarf.

The *Monitor* and the *Merrimack* fight their historic duel at Hampton Roads.

Dr. Edward Shippen, the surgeon who had been aboard the *Congress,* watched from the shore. He described the initial attack by the *Monitor* on the *Merrimack,* as looking "like a big, hulking bully suddenly attacked by a plucky, determined little man." Around and around they circled each other, like boxers dancing between punches. The air was filled with fire and smoke, and the spectators on the banks had trouble seeing through the thick haze. The other ships scattered.

On the deck of the *Merrimack,* there was "the noise of the crackling, roaring fires, escaping steam, and the loud and labored pulsations of the engines, together with the roar of battle above and the thud and vibration of the huge masses of iron being hurled against her sides." The crew had some trouble seeing their opponent because of the billowing smoke on deck and the diminutive size of the *Monitor.* The *Merrimack* was now leaking badly. The added weight of water in the hold, which could not be adequately pumped out, made it difficult to maneuver the ship. "Our ship was working worse and worse," John Wood sadly declared.

L. Catesby Jones, executive officer on the *Merrimack,* observed, "The *Monitor* and her turret appeared to be under perfect control. Her light draft enabled her to move about us at pleasure. She once took position for a short time when we could not bring a gun to bear on her."

Captain Van Brunk, watching from the deck of the *Minnesota* observed that "Gun after gun was fired by the *Monitor* which was returned with whole broadsides by the rebels with no more effect, apparently, than so many pebblestones thrown by a child."

A newspaper reporter, watching through a long spy glass, wrote, "The *Monitor* spun around like a top and, as she got her bearing again, sent one of her formidable missiles into her huge opponent." All the people present agreed that it was an amazing sight. One of the spectators, James Stephens, wrote:

> All in all, it was a thrilling scene. In the foreground lay a magnificent ship, an alluring stake in the contest. Immense volumes of smoke rolled away from her decks as she rained ponderous balls upon her would-be captor. To the left was the Fortress Monroe and in the background Sewell's Point, their parapets and beach crowded with interested spectators. Hovering on the outskirts at a safe distance were numbers of Union and Rebel vessels. In the center the attraction of all eyes were the two ironclads grappling as in a life and death struggle, the one maneuvering for position to rake the strange ship, the other rushing in to make her change position and defeat the project.

On the deck of the *Monitor,* the crew of 59 men was more calm. Several shots had dented the ship's sides, but they had not penetrated the ship. It was intact. The *Monitor* was easier to maneuver than its opponent. It sat very low in the water, and, because of its rotating turret, was quicker on the draw. The *Monitor* was a hard target for the enemy to see. Time after time, the *Merrimack*'s crew thought that the strange little warship had been sunk to the bottom of the river, and time after time it kept reappearing when the smoke cleared.

Finally, in desperation, the commanding officer of the *Merrimack* gave the order to ram the *Monitor*. He was not aware that this ship no longer had its iron ram. It had lost it in battle the day before. Both ships readied themselves for the coming blow. Then, at the last minute, commanding officer Jones changed his order. He was afraid of too great an impact. His ship did not ram the *Monitor* at full speed, only at half speed. The jarring blow was severe, but it was not fatal.

After this attack, the crews returned to their guns, and never stopped firing. "The noise of every solid ball that hit fell upon our ears with a crash that deafened us," reported quartermaster Peter Truscott aboard the *Monitor*.

The *Monitor* finally moved out of sight in order to reload its turret. It steamed to shallow water, where the enemy could not follow. The *Merrimack* took aim at the *Minnesota* once again. But the *Monitor*, turning its guns around, was ready with a few last shots. One of the crew on the *Minnesota* remarked that "it was really laughable. The *Merrimack* was making strenuous efforts to get down to us, but always just before her was the diminutive 'Pill Box' waiting every chance and putting in a shot at each."

One of the Confederate seamen decided to jump aboard "the bloody little iron tub." But before he could, the *Monitor* had steamed past and the chance was lost. The commanding officer then ordered his gunners to fire on the *Monitor*'s pilothouse. That would be the most likely target to destroy. The gunners obeyed, but they did not succeed in destroying the pilothouse. However, they did blind J. L. John Worden, commander of the *Monitor*. "Save the *Minnesota* if you can" were Worden's last words before he was taken below.

The *Minnesota* was saved, partly because the tide was running out and the *Merrimack* was forced to retreat to deeper waters. But the main reason it was saved was "the funny little tin box on a raft." Leaking badly and with a very tired crew, the Confederate ship headed back to Norfolk for repairs. It had been hit hundreds of times in two days of fighting. Neither ship had won the battle, but both ships claimed victory.

At Forth Monroe, Captain Fox prepared his telegram for Gideon Welles. It read:

The *Monitor* arrived at 10 P.M. last night and went immediately to the protection of the *Minnesota,* lying aground just below Newport News. At 7 A.M. today the *Merrimack,* accompanied by two wooden steamers and several tugs, stood out toward the *Minnesota* and opened fire. The *Monitor* met them at once and opened her fire, when all the enemy's vessels retired, excepting the *Merrimack.* These two ironclad vessels fought part of the time touching each other, from 8 A.M. to noon, when the *Merrimack* retired. Whether she is injured or not it is impossible to say. Lieutenant J. L. Worden, who commanded the *Monitor,* handled her with great skill, assisted by Chief Engineer Stimers. Lieutenant Worden was injured by the cement from the pilot house being driven into his eyes, but I trust not seriously. The *Minnesota* kept up a continuous fire and is herself somewhat injured. She was moved considerably today, and will probably be off tonight. The *Monitor* is uninjured and ready at any moment to repel another attack.

On shore, the spectators, who had watched the battle for four hours, termed the encounter a "great success." John Ericsson did not. He firmly believed that the *Monitor* should have sunk the *Merrimack* in 15 minutes. He blamed the crew for a performance that fell far short of his expectations. "Even so, the little *Monitor* had proved her ability. She hit the *Virginia* 50 times, cracking six of the bigger ship's iron plates, and sent her home leaking. She had been hit only 21 times herself, and was virtually undamaged."

The *Monitor* joined the Union fleet for a two-month rest at Hampton Roads before sailing south to North Carolina to assist in a Union attack. However, it ran into a violent storm off Cape Hatteras and sank.

The *Merrimack* also had a sad ending. After being repaired, it was sent back into action in Virginia. As the Union armies advanced, the threat of its capture became likely. Its commander, Commodore Josiah Tattnall, then gave the order to run it aground and set it on fire. When the flames reached its ammunition, the ship exploded.

Although "the greatest duel of naval history" had ended in a draw, John Ericsson's "floating battery" had held the Union blockade together. The "tin box on a raft" had revolutionized naval warfare.

THE REVOLUTION IN THE NAVIES

"Those damn teakettles ..."

FLAG OFFICER DAVID FARRAGUT

The years leading up to the Civil War were already a time of tremendous changes in shipbuilding technology. It was the war that focused that technology on the building of a new kind of warship. At the beginning of the war, most ships were wooden-hulled and powered by sails. Four years later, the standard navy vessel was an ironclad ship operating on steam power. Wars have always encouraged technological advances. Men like John Ericsson found the Civil War an opportunity to bring about a revolution in sea power.

The navies of the North and South had very different resources available to them when the war broke out. The South had few ships, and none of these were first-class fighting vessels. The North had a navy of 100 ships. Many of these were old-fashioned or badly in need of repair, but the North had the facilities to get these vessels into shape quickly. The South lacked factories and shipyards, so it had to be very creative if it was to develop any kind of navy.

One of the things the Southern leaders did was to look abroad for help with its navy. England was officially neutral in the

American Civil War, but Jefferson Davis, the president of the Confederacy, knew that England secretly hoped that the North would lose the war. He had his secretary of the navy, Stephen Mallory, strike a deal with English shipbuilding firms. They would produce several sleek warships, powered both by sails and steam, for the Confederacy. Officially, the British were not allowed to aid the Confederacy with military hardware. The foreign firms got around this by equipping the ships with everything except guns, which would be mounted later. Union spies saw the ships being built, saw the gun mounts in place, and knew that England was aiding the Confederacy in violation of international law. But by the time the U.S. government's complaints were answered, the ships were built and sailing for the Confederacy.

The Confederate leaders knew they could never assemble a complete navy to rival the Union's vessels, so they took a different approach. The Union's strategy was to blockade Southern ports with the many ships it had gathered together. The Confederate leaders knew that most of these Union vessels were wooden ships. If the Confederacy could build a few ironclad rams, these could be used to punch holes in the Union blockade lines.

The Laird ram, built by the British shipbuilders of the same name, was a technological innovation that went beyond Ericsson's *Monitor* in its impact on the war. In fact, the *Monitor* was more significant for what it gave to the future of naval technology than for what it accomplished during the war. The Laird ram, however, had immediate and profound effects on the war. Attached to the front of a powerful wooden–hulled ship, the ram could be a devastating offensive weapon. Armed with the rams, Confederate ships could drive into wooden Union vessels and sink them handily.

Nevertheless, as the war progressed, the Union's greater strength and technological superiority swung the balance in its favor. The blockade of Southern ports was working. Southern cities could not receive goods from Europe or from other Southern cities via sea. The South was slowly being choked off from the world.

Ironclad rams like this one, the C.S.S. *Manassas*, helped the Confederacy to resist the Union blockade.

Stephen Mallory cast about for other ways to strike at the Union. He organized teams of the South's best sailors for a dangerous but thrilling mission: blockade running. These sailors manned small, sleek ships whose purpose was to slip past the slower blockading ships into the open waters. From there, they were to proceed to neutral ports, often in the Caribbean, load up with supplies, and then return home. The final stage was to dash back through the line of blockading vessels and deliver their precious cargoes of much-needed goods.

Blockade running paid well and offered sailors excitement. But it was also a very dangerous business. The Union captured more than 1,000 blockade runners during the course of the war. Thousands of daring soldiers lost their lives attempting to run the blockade.

Stephen Mallory had one other tactic for attacking the Union by sea. Against the hundreds of vessels that now comprised the Union navy, he put a single ship. It was called the *Alabama*. Over the

Admiral David Dixon Porter, who led the gunboats at the battle of Vicksburg, supported the development of ironclads.

course of 22 months, this one vessel nearly brought Union shipping to a halt.

The *Alabama* was one of the ships Mallory had had built in England. It was a model of Civil War naval technology. It had both a steam engine and powerful sails, so that it could go on long voyages without refueling, taking advantage of wind power. Its hull was narrow, cutting down on wind resistance and enabling it to fly across the waves like an arrow.

But perhaps the most important feature of the *Alabama* was not a technological one. It was its captain. Raphael Semmes was considered by many to be the ablest sailor in the South. He was brash, daring, and ingenious, and he hated the North. Semmes assembled a ragtag crew from the Liverpool docks, where the *Alabama* was constructed, and set off on an around-the-world journey.

The *Alabama's* mission was to destroy Union commerce at sea. Over the 22-month period of its mission, the *Alabama* destroyed or captured 68 ships. Readers of newspapers in the North found almost daily accounts of the ravages this one ship was making on their commerce. The *Alabama* would be sighted in the Caribbean, seemingly heading north toward Florida. Then it was reported to have sunk a dozen Union whaling vessels off the coast of South America. Next it turned up off the coast of India, then in the South Pacific.

President Lincoln sent ship after ship in search of the *Alabama*. It was finally caught off the coast of France by the U.S.S. *Kearsarge*. The two ships fought a dazzling sea battle, which brought spectators all the way from Paris. In the end, the *Alabama* was sunk. Semmes, however, escaped into an English yacht that was in the harbor to view the battle, and eventually returned to the South to fight once again for his beloved Confederacy.

The Union navy continued to grow in strength throughout the war. A fleet under the command of Admiral David Farragut sailed through the Gulf of Mexico to the mouth of the Mississippi River. From there, Farragut attacked and subdued the city of New Orleans, the largest city in the South. He then proceeded upriver,

Admiral David Farragut proved adept at the use of the new naval technology, though he did not fully approve of it.

sealing off the Mississippi from Southern use and further tightening the stranglehold on the Confederacy.

Farragut, an old veteran who had first fought in the War of 1812, was uncomfortable with the newfangled changes being brought about by men like John Ericsson. He did not like the idea of ironclad vessels. "When a shell makes its way into one of those damn teakettles," he once said, "it can't get out again. It sputters around inside doing all kinds of mischief." In one important encounter, however, even Farragut adopted the idea of metal covering for his ships. During the Battle of New Orleans, Farragut's ships had to pass two forts that guarded the harbor entrance. Farragut had his ships' hulls covered with iron chains to form a protective covering. With this "coat of armor," the ships passed the forts successfully.

Another significant advance in naval technology that the Civil War brought was the submarine. The first sub was called a "Hunley" after its inventor, Horace Hunley. People who saw it said it looked like a floating cigar. Hunley's first several ships sank, killing many crewmen. But finally, in 1863, a "Hunley" met a Confederate ship in battle, and the submarine fired a blast that sank the ship. Unfortunately, the "Hunley" sank at the same time. The crude vessel did not contribute to the Union navy during the Civil War, but it did represent an important stage in engineering history.

THE ACHIEVER

> "And you will someday produce something extraordinary."
>
> COUNT VON PLATEN
> TO ERICSSON

An old man sat alone in a room in lower Manhattan. It was 24 years since the Civil War had ended, and John Ericsson was 86 years old. The tall pine trees of his youth in Sweden had been replaced by New York's tall buildings. The lights and shadows fell not on a quiet forest but on busy, crowded streets. The mist that had hung gently over the Swedish streams was now puffing smoke rising skyward from the East River. New York was the center of industry that John Ericsson had helped to develop.

After the war had come Reconstruction. Ericsson had watched it all happen. The United States was rich now. It was selling more goods than it was buying from other countries. It was truly an independent nation. Inventions that were once only toys were now being mass-produced and sent all over the world. The telephone and the telegraph carried messages to every continent. The world was much smaller now, with what seemed like endless opportunities ahead.

"I tell you these are great times," the historian Henry Adams stated.

Man has mounted science, and [science has] now run away with [him]. I firmly believe that before many centuries more, science

will be the master of man. The engines he will have invented will
be beyond his strength to control. Some day science may have the
existence of mankind in its power, and the human race commit
suicide by blowing up the world. Not only shall we be able to
cruise in space, but I see no reason why some future generation
shouldn't walk off like a beetle with the world on its back.

John Ericsson must have believed all this. After all, he had surely
contributed to that creed. He had introduced the first screw-
propelled warship that was driven by steam, and the age of paddle-
driven sailing ships was finished. He had invented the revolving
turret on an ironclad warship, and the age of the wooden men-of-
war was over. The old shot and shell ammunition was now
obsolete, and more effective and deadly weapons would have to be
found. All these contributions made by John Ericsson paved the
way for the 20th century "battleship," the class of warship fitted
with the most powerful armament available and displaying the
most striking force in naval warfare all over the world.

Ericsson never gave up on his questions and his dreams. He
never stopped believing in himself, in spite of the damaging
remarks of some critics throughout his lifetime. Concerning one of
those critics, he once said:

> The bitter and unjust remarks of the editor of *The Engineer* are only
> a repetition of what I have experienced through life, simply from
> the fact that in my profession I know more than most other people.
> Not one in a hundred of those critics who assailed me, and by their
> injustice rendered a life otherwise fortunate, often very unpleasant,
> would have done so had their experience and knowledge not been
> inferior to mine. It is my consolation, however, to feel that those
> only who do not know me accuse me of ignorance in my
> profession, and that those who know me best have least to say
> against me.

The walls of Ericsson's house were covered with honorary
degrees from all over the world. The tables were covered with
models of his inventions and scientific books. His desk was covered
with invitations for speaking engagements and exhibition
openings.

Ericsson had always been interested in attending exhibitions. In fact, about the only time that he left his house was to attend some sort of exhibition. He found exhibitions to be stimulating and inspiring and always a pleasant experience—with one exception. That was the Philadelphia Centennial Exhibition of 1876. He had been asked only to contribute turret drawings of his *Monitor.* His achievements in other areas had been completely ignored. This angered him. However, he decided to attend the exhibition, and the occasion resulted in a meeting with the son he had never seen.

Hjalmar Elworth, by then a noted Swedish engineer and superintendent of the Swedish State Railroad, had been appointed to represent his government at the exhibition. The meeting between Ericsson and his son was cordial but restrained. The two men had very different personalities. The son believed in being "mild in words and strong in deeds." The father believed that "the hammer is my weapon." However, Ericsson was proud of his son's accomplishments and later showed his affection by sending him gifts of stocks and securities.

Ericsson seemed unable to show love and affection in any other way—he certainly could not do it with words. When Elworth died of Bright's disease in 1887, Ericsson wrote to his daughter-in-law:

My dear Sophie:
The account in your letter of May 25th, concerning Hjalmar's dreadful state, was painful beyond description. I received, therefore, the telegram that afterward came from Baron Ericsson with more satisfaction than grief, as death alone could ease your husband's pains. His constitution was evidently completely destroyed by physician's ignorance and his own senselessness. The fact is that your husband, who was an unusually strong man, was simply murdered by ignorance. Please give my thanks to your sister for her clear account of the funeral. Grand funerals are objectionable to my opinion, but in this case it was friendship that arranged the unnecessary pomp.

Your affectionate friend,

J. Ericsson

This letter could hardly have consoled his son's widow. Ericsson, many years before, had broken family ties. His brother, Nils, had changed the spelling of his name to Ericson, in order to distance himself from a man he considered to be an "impractical and debt-ridden father: and an equally impractical brother." John's sister, Anna, and the mother he had loved so much, were both gone.

Ericsson's work was all that mattered to him. In his later years, he was mainly concerned with the letters he received from young inventors asking for his advice and direction. He always answered these letters quickly and in great detail. After all, these letters asked the questions of the future.

His home was still the laboratory and workshop in which Amelia had felt unwelcome. Ericsson heard of her death, after a short illness, in England in 1867. He said of his marriage, "Fate, by this misalliance, made it possible for me to devote 25 years of undivided, undisturbed attention to work, which would not have been so if I lived in what is called a happy marriage."

The success of the *Monitor* had created a great demand for ships of its type. The ship had proved incapable of standing up to heavy seas, but orders came in from all over the world for more and more ships like it to be used in calm inland waterways as river gunboats. In fact, until World War I, *Monitor*-type ironclad vessels continued to patrol inland waters.

In spite of the *Monitor's* popularity, however, it was no longer considered an effective "engine of war." It was no longer worthy of Ericsson's attention. The United States Navy was now talking about a "movable torpedo" or underwater missile. This idea was not new. The ancient Greeks had thought about it, and the French had tried to develop it the century before. Robert Fulton had tried in 1810. Samuel Colt had advanced ideas about one in 1842. Ericsson had even considered the possibility of an underwater missile 25 years earlier. It would use compressed air for power.

He submitted his plan to the navy for "a torpedo 25 feet long, weighing some 1,500 pounds, capable of carrying an explosive charge of 320 pounds of powder. It would be movable and subaqueous, controlled by a tubular cable and propelled by

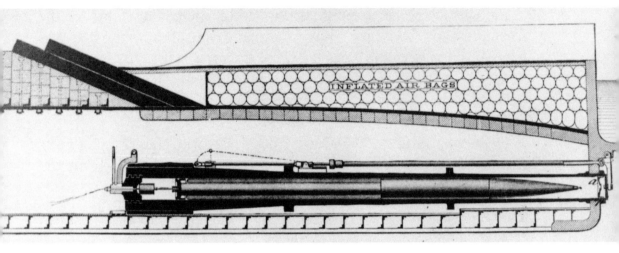

INFLATED AIR BAGS

The torpedo was yet another Ericsson invention that would later transform naval warfare.

compressed air." The torpedo would be dispatched from a horizontal tube through the submerged part of a ship's hull, and it anticipated the submarine. The ship was called the *Destroyer*.

The U.S. Navy was reluctant to support this new venture. The navy had spent too much money during the Civil War. Even Ericsson's friend Cornelius Delamater was hesitant. He too, was running out of funds for speculation. So Ericsson took his case to his old opponent, the British Admiralty. To his surprise, they agreed to give it a trial. Also to his surprise, it failed. It was a sad irony that it should fail in the waters of England, where Ericsson's ideas had been rejected so many times. After his death, however, the *Destroyer* made good its promise during a brief civil war in Brazil.

Although most historians say John Ericsson's greatest contribution was "the cannon in the revolving turret," Ericsson felt differently. He had devoted his life to heat as the ultimate form of energy. War, unfortunately, had altered his goal. He wrote to a friend that "the satisfaction with which I lay my head on the pillow at night, conscious of having through my small caloric engine conferred a boon on mankind...is far greater than the satisfaction the production of an engine of war can give."

Perhaps for that reason, he had given up the patent rights for the *Monitor*. And with those rights, he had given up a fortune. It was probably not Ericsson's usual lack of business sense that persuaded him to give up ownership of the *Monitor* patents. It may have been because of his moral beliefs. Ericsson was convinced that war was wrong.

However, with the war over and the world clamoring for his *Monitor* design, he was able to collect substantial funds from the

Naval historians consider the revolving cannon turret, one of which is shown here, to be Ericsson's greatest invention.

production of the ship as well as from many of his other inventions. For the first time in his life, he was financially independent.

Ericsson employed a staff of five people. Two assistants and a secretary looked after his business affairs, and a housekeeper and a cook looked after his house. There was also a widow named Sarah Thorn, 12 years younger than Ericsson, who was his steady companion for many years after the Civil War. Her relationship with him remains a mystery, except that she was an old friend whom he helped support financially and whom he probably loved. Unlike his late wife, this woman must have been able to cope with the oddities of an inventor who lived entirely for his work. These were the only people that he saw now, except for his old friend, Delamater, and an admiring neighbor named Charles Harris.

In quiet solitude, with enough time and money at his disposal, he picked up his drawing board once again. He asked himself more questions. How could solar energy be used? What is the value of radiant heat—heat that spreads out in rays from a central source?

He built an observatory on the roof of his house, and he went to work. The result was the invention of seven motors which were activated by the heat of the sun. He showed one of them to Harris and said proudly that he called it his solar "furnace." Then he hurried on to explain that,

> turned up as you see it, and exposed to the rays of the run, the light is concentrated on the metal tube containing water. The concentrated rays generate heat, acting like a burning glass. The water is converted into steam which, conveyed through the attached pipe, moves this little engine. It may be only a toy, power depending on the size of the generator, but the fact that it requires no fuel but sunlight, free to all, is its great advantage.

He had never forgotten the simple experiment that his father had shown him back in Sweden, 80 years before. Heat can cause motion.

The sun motors worked well in the hot summer months, but he was unable to store solar energy in the winter. So, resourceful as

always, he merely turned the engine upside down and ran it on coal, gas, or wood. It was an instant success, used for pumping water and running all kinds of small equipment. Delamater's company got the rewards, since Ericsson, once again, had neglected to obtain a patent.

He never stopped dreaming and studying and questioning. He never ceased to learn about scientific principles. Yet he seemed unable to learn about business practices. He never learned to protect his inventions. Nor did he receive the recognition he deserved for his contributions to science and technology.

Finally, because of ill health and the need to have doctors and nurses constantly at his side in his old age, he was again without much money.

John Ericsson died of a kidney disease on May 8, 1889. His body was returned to Sweden, at the request of the Swedish government. He was buried in Vermland, at Filipstad, on September 15, 1890.

At a ceremony in New York harbor aboard the U.S.S. *Baltimore,*

John Ericsson was most proud of his non-military inventions, and yet he was famous for his machines of war.

John Ericsson's body was surrounded by officials and an honor guard. The Swedish flag waved brightly in the hot August sun, and a 21-gun salute shook the deck of the steamship as it glided swiftly through the Narrows—past schooners, sloops, ferryboats, tugboats, steamships, and warships, all flying the United States flag at half-mast. Ericsson would probably have described the occasion as "unnecessary pomp," but he would have been pleased by the pride and affection that was shown.

George H. Robinson of the Delamater Iron Works, spoke for his father-in-law, the late Cornelius Delamater, and for John Ericsson's adopted country:

In the nation's tribute to our illustrious dead the simple duty falls to us to yield to the claims of his mother country, that she may again receive her son. We send him back crowned with honor; proud of the life of fifty years he devoted to his nation, and with gratitude for the gifts he gave us. Was he a dreamer? Yes. He dreamed of the practical application of screw-propulsion, and the commerce of the world was revolutionized. He dreamed of making naval warfare more terrible, and the *Monitor* was built.... Again he dreamed, and the *Destroyer*, with its submarine gun, was born. He dreamed of hot air, and behold 10,000 caloric engines. He dreamed of the sun's rays in sandy deserts, where water was hard to get, and the solar engine came.... To you, Captain Schley, we commit these remains. The honorable duty is yours. Deliver them to his native country. We keep his memory here.

TIMETABLE OF EVENTS IN THE LIFE OF
JOHN ERICSSON

July 31, 1803	Born in Varmland, Sweden
1816	Appointed as cadet in the mechanical corps of the Swedish navy
1818	Father, Olaf Ericsson, dies
1824	Son, Hjalmar Elworth, born
1826	Travels to England to demonstrate flame engine Becomes partner with John Braithwaite
1829	Invents surface condenser Develops locomotive engine *Novelty*
1836	Marries Amelia Byam Invents screw propeller
1839	Moves to United States
1841	Pioneers design for first screw-propelled warship
1843	His warship *Princeton* launched, winning a contest with the British *Great Western*
1844	Robert Stockton's addition of "Peacemaker" gun causes an explosion on the *Princeton*
1846	Sends design of raftlike warship with engine beneath the waterline to Congress
1848	Becomes American citizen
1851	Displays some of his inventions at London's Crystal Palace Exhibition
1861	Proposes to President Lincoln to build an iron battleship with caloric power
1862	The *Monitor* saves Union blockade in the most famous naval battle of the Civil War
1867	Wife, Amelia, dies
1876	Exhibits *Monitor* drawings at Philadelphia Centennial Exhibition Meets son
March 8, 1889	Dies in New York

Suggested Reading

Catton, Bruce. *The Civil War.* New York: Houghton Mifflin, 1987 (originally published 1960).

Donovan, Frank. *Ironclads of the Civil War.* New York: American Heritage, 1964.

Kismaric, Carole. *Duel of the Ironclads.* New York: Time-Life Books, 1969.

MacBride, Robert. *Civil War Ironclads.* Philadelphia: Chilton, 1962.

*Pratt, Fletcher. *The Monitor and the Merrimack.* New York: Random House, 1951.

*White, William C. and Ruth. *Tin Can on a Shingle.* New York: Dutton, 1958.

*Readers of *John Ericsson: The Inventions of War* will find these books particularly readable.

SELECTED SOURCES

Chapelle, Howard I. *The American Sailing Navy.* New York: Norton, 1949.

Church, William Conant. *The Life of John Ericsson.* New York: Holt, 1960.

Davis, William C. *Duel Between the First Ironclads.* New York: Doubleday, 1975.

Foote, Shelby. *The Civil War.* New York: Random House, 1958.

Hart, Roger. *English Life in the Nineteenth Century.* New York: Putnam, 1971.

Heidenstam, O.G. *Swedish Life in Town and Country.* New York: Putnam, 1904.

Hoehling, A.A. *Thunder at Hampton Roads.* Englewood Cliffs, N.J.: Prentice Hall, 1976.

Husband, Joseph. *American by Adoption.* Boston: Atlantic Monthly Press, 1920.

Landstrom, Bjorn. *The Ship.* Garden City, N.Y.: Doubleday, 1961.

Leckie, Robert. *The Wars of America.* New York: Harper & Row, 1968.

Macintyre, Donald, and Basil W. Bathe. *Man-of-War, A History of the Combat Vessel.* New York: McGraw-Hill, 1969.

Osborne, John W. *The Silent Revolution.* New York: Charles Scribner's Sons, 1970.

Trager, James. *The People's Chronology.* New York: Holt, Rinehart & Winston, 1979.

White, Ruth. *Yankee from Sweden.* New York: Holt, 1960.

Index

Ann Brophy teaches writing for children at Fairfield University. She has written poetry, short stories, young adult novels and a nonfiction book on the battle of Gettysburg. Currently, she is at work on a middle-grade mystery novel and a picture book. Ms. Brophy is the mother of three grown children and lives in Southport, Connecticut, with her husband.